Counter Culture

An Essential Guide for Service

Joshua Farrell

COPYRIGHT

Counter Culture: An Essential Guide for Service

Copyright © 2023 by Joshua Farrell

Published in the United States by Schellville.

Contact Email: info@schellvillepublishing.com

ISBN: 978-0-9899345-1-0

Edited by Elizabeth Bagby

Cover Design: Christo Downs

"I've learned that people will forget what you said, people will forget what you did, but people will never forget how you made them feel."

-Maya Angelou

CONTENTS

INTRODUCTION

A thing I loved about growing up in a small town is that when you went to the store you almost always had an interaction as opposed to a transaction with the people working there. I grew up accustomed to people at the counter at Safeway grocery store, The Bagel Shop, or Pinelli Hardware who would look you in the eye and honestly ask, "How are you?" or say, "Good morning." A brief moment, a smile, or a kind word. And if I didn't already know the person, that is how I got to know them. I remembered them, I had a pleasant feeling associated with the person, and that alone set them apart from the rest.

I'm going to guess that there are people in your life, outside of work, who are special to you because of the way they engage with you. That type of engaging is what makes them stand out from others. A favorite aunt, a lifelong friend, an amazing teacher, or a coach. When you see them, they engage with you, say hi, remember something about you, and look genuinely happy to see you. They make you feel good. Connected. You might trust them more than others or know you can depend on them in certain situations. That connection and trust is what hospitality is all about.

Hospitality

Dictionary.com defines hospitality as "the friendly and generous reception and entertainment of guests, visitors, or strangers." If you have picked up this book, it may be because you have a sense that counter service within the hospitality industry is different from other types of counter service. That counter service within food and beverage businesses, a part of the hospitality industry, is something more than a forgettable transaction at your local convenience store, doctor's office, or bank. Stop today, take a moment when you are in a line, and watch the interaction that is taking place in front of you at a counter. Anywhere. Just notice it. You will be quite surprised that not all places are created equal. Not all counter servers take the time to interact and say hi to their guests.

Counter service should be a "friendly and generous" interaction, but frankly, it's just not. People ring customers up at the counter without even saying a word — no hello, no eye contact, coming across bothered that you are even there. Being friendly and generous is a choice that isn't taken every day. You shouldn't have to be in hospitality to know that you should be friendly and generous to someone who is actively choosing to spend their money to pay for a product or service. You shouldn't have to hope to get the "nice" person at the counter.

Let's take three scenarios of a simple task. Let's say I had to simply bring you a cookie on a plate:

- **I could just slide the plate in front of you and walk away.**

- **I could place the plate in front of you, smile and say, "Here's your cookie."**

- **I could lightly place the plate in front of you, smile and say, "Good afternoon, here is your warm chocolate chip cookie. Is there anything else I can bring out for you?"**

One task, three different ways. Which way feels friendly and generous to you? This book will offer some guidance on how to engage well with your guests, your co-workers, your employees, and your boss, as well as introduce you to some amazing people who work in counter service.

Our Guest

I like to use the word *guest* instead of *customer*. They refer to the same person, but using the word *guest* gives me a different intention with that person. It makes me want to be of service to the guest, meet them with my hospitality, and not just wait for them to wander around the store to find me.

When I was a kid, my parents had guests over a lot for dinner and for parties. We didn't have customers, we had people over who we connected with and knew, or came to know, and developed relationships with. When I think of a customer, I just think of someone pulling a ticket number from the wheel and waiting for someone behind a counter to yell for that number. This isn't us. That's not hospitality, and it isn't how we do counter service. These are some of the things that set us apart. By using the word *guest*, we enter a contract with ourselves to treat all of our customers as true guests. So...guests it is!

The Craft

I grew up working in our family lumberyard and on construction crews. I learned construction through craftsmen, the guys who took pride in teaching the new person the right way to do things. With a lot of direction and feedback, I acquired the skills to cut wood, build trusses, hang drywall, frame a house, and pour concrete to build a foundation. I was able to absorb all of this from listening to my bosses and senior workers on the crew, making mistakes, asking questions, and honing my skills until the attention to details became second nature. I learned how to drive a forklift before a car. (Made more than my share of mistakes on that forklift!)

This same method of learning followed me through my pursuit of education, arts, and hospitality. I've grasped everything I know from people I've worked for, the people I worked with, and the books they've recommended to me. It was these gracious people in restaurant service who took me under their wings at one point or another and showed me how it was done and what the expectations were. That a craftsperson needed to meet a standard. The duty and honor of a craftsperson isn't just to do your job, but to do your job well. Consistently. Over and over again.

Learning

You could do a job behind a counter and pay no attention to anything that I've described above, make a paycheck, and get through the day. You'd be fine. Maybe a little bored. The great thing about a hospitality mindset is that you always have options to be better and hone your skills. If you commit to the tenants of good service and executing them day in and day out, you will see a transformation in yourself. You have that option every day in hospitality. There is a reason you are holding this book in your hand right now. You can grow daily and hone the skills that will help you in all areas of your life. I've truly enjoyed learning all of the following working in hospitality:

- **Learning to read a room**

- **Multi-tasking**

- **Talking to people of different backgrounds**

- **Learning to take direction**

- **Accepting constructive feedback**

- **Communicating with many types of people**

- **Meeting new people and friends**

- **How to read nonverbal communication**

- **Learning time management skills and responsibilities**

- Selling products and gaining product knowledge

- Understanding different people and viewpoints

Blondie's Pizza

My first experience working behind the counter was when I was living and going to school in San Francisco in my early twenties. I worked at Blondie's Pizza at the Powell Street cable car turnaround—a tourist-busy spot a couple of blocks off of Union Square.

I had needed a gig on the weekends, so I dropped off a résumé and got a call. It was a simple service place. The guest walks up to the counter, orders a slice of pizza or a whole pie, pays the cashier, waits for their name to be called, and their food is handed to them. It was a tiny room. We had a small counter lining the wall where you could eat while standing. Very similar to a lot of New York slice shops.

My duties were pretty straightforward. I started as a cashier and worked at that position for a couple of months, and then joined the rotation of making dough and assembling pizzas. Eventually, I made it up to working a few shifts cooking the pizzas in the oven. Being that cook was the sought-after position. But I preferred talking with people at the register. It was more fun, and I would meet random people from everywhere. My manager at the time was a cool guy and was always impressed with my positive energy, interacting with guests and my co-workers.

It was a super-busy spot. We would get swamped in waves. Each cashier had their own line, and oftentimes you were looking at eight or nine people in your line, ten to fifteen if it was a rush. Service moved fast! People could be very testy by the time they arrived at the front of the line, but we used a lot of humor, and most of the people who I worked with on the registers were pretty great when it came to dealing with guests. Interaction with guests was highly encouraged!

The guest had three types of pizza to choose from, so it wasn't too difficult explaining the concept and ingredients. But you did have people make specific requests, so making sure the correct information got to the assembler and the cook was very important. A mistake would put the cooks in the weeds and make our waiting times even longer. We didn't have the advantage of an advanced computer system, so communication was super-important.

My favorite part of the job was the people: the people I worked with and the random types of people, from all walks of life, who would appear at the counter out of the San Francisco fog, hungry for a slice of pizza. The people I worked with made the job. It was such a diverse crew. Leonard had moved from Detroit and had his own start-up business; there was a college student from Toronto, a DJ who grew up a few blocks away, and a manager who had late-night gigs as a go-go dancer. We represented many different races and cultures. Most of us were in our twenties pursuing other things: school, art, side businesses. We laughed a lot, had fun, worked fast and hard, made our money—and got to take a little pizza home at the end of the shift!

My manager, Steve, was great with my schedule. I could only work on the weekends because of school, so I would work my eight-hour shifts on each Saturday and Sunday and then occasionally pick up Friday nights and weeknight shifts if I had a break in my evening studies. This was perfect for me because a lot of my co-workers wanted weekends off. But I did have to remain flexible: I was the new guy. The job didn't pay a lot of money, but it gave me enough to cover some bills and take a girl on a date here and there.

Obviously, the money was important, but the fun we had at work was what made the job enjoyable for me, and that energy was passed on to the guest. And those people came back as repeat guests. We were hustling, interacting with people, getting pizzas out quick, and maintaining a friendly, fun vibe all at the same time. All four of those elements are essential in counter service. And service was really quick, one minute with a guest at the counter—a fast interaction with a quick "hello" or conversation.

Friendly and Engaging

Fast food, fast casual, and coffee bars are all similar in that you only have this short amount of time to greet the guest, make an impression, answer some questions about the products you serve, take their order, process the payment, instruct them on how they will get the order, and say goodbye. Being friendly and connecting with the guest is essential during this brief interaction. If you aren't friendly, it can easily seem transactional, with no feeling. And that is a challenge for a restaurant and for you.

Employers want friendly people to work for them and engage with guests. Ultimately, a positive employee who can engage in a friendly way with co-workers and guests, multitask, stay focused, and keep that energy consistent throughout a full eight-hour shift is someone they are going to want to hire and promote, and someone they will be excited to work with.

A Conversation Starter

My hope for this book is that it answers some questions for you, that a few of the ideas and tools jump out at you, make sense, and spark some interest. I'm not the last word on the subject; I'm just one of many.

In all of my service jobs, the thing I liked—and still do to this day—is asking, "How can we do it better?" How can we offer a unique perspective that still serves the guest first? How can we push the limits? Discussing these questions and many more, hanging out after work or during service, was always a pleasure for me. So, if you hate something in here, cool. Talk about it. If you love something in here, great. Talk about it. And if you're burned out from work and don't feel like reading, put this book down and turn on a ballgame. Enjoy!

This book is meant to be a conversation starter! What service means to you, your co-workers, your employees, your customers. This book is meant to inspire a conversation that you can have with people who are driven by good service. Service is different for every place of business. It's not one-size-fits-all. Yes, there are elements of service that should never be missed, but my hope is you will take what works for you, build on those elements you like, and create better ways to serve your guests through your own discussions and innovations.

> **So, if you hate something in here, cool. Talk about it. If you love something in here, great. Talk about it. And if you're burned out from work and don't feel like reading, put this book down and turn on a ballgame. Enjoy!**

If you are reading this book and you find yourself saying, "This dude completely missed asking questions about holding the door open for guests or wiping down chairs on the patio," good! Great! That means this book is working. It's to get you to start asking yourself, how can you be of service? How can you improve what you are doing? And how can you innovate and continue to exceed your customers' expectations? That is the conversation that always needs to be happening, both inside your head and with others.

Repetition and Retention

There is going to be some repetition in this book. I say that because some of the same notes about service I received at Blondie's Pizza, I received working in a Michelin-starred fine dining restaurant. We are always reminding each other of some of the most important and basic elements of service regardless of where we work. I've heard these consistently in every hospitality job I've had:

- **Say hi to the guests**

- **Don't cross your arms on the floor**

- **Try to use the guest's name**

- **Don't forget to put guest's allergies into the order**

- **Check your order before you hit Send**

- **Pre-bus your tables**

- **Say goodbye to the guest**

There are many more notes that you will hear moving through different jobs in hospitality. These are important points, and you will hear them at any place that is determined to deliver good service to guests. You will hear them in this book over and over because servers can forget some of the most basic tenets of service at any style of restaurant you may be working at. It's just part of the commitment to the craft.

Looking for a Job

"Where do I find information on looking for a job? I've never been good at interviews and don't know what to expect." If you are interested in finding a job in counter service, I have included its own section in the back of the book. It's titled, "How to get Hired." You will find many tips about being prepared, what to expect from the interview process, even what to wear.

How to Use this Book

You can read this book front to back, or you can simply look for a very specific subject from the Contents section in the front of the book or the Index section in the back of the book. If you've had some experience and are trying to brush up on some skills, jump around and find a topic that motivates you or makes you nervous. There is plenty of wisdom, thoughts, and advice from other amazing people throughout this book. This may be a guide you are using to find your first job; you may be a new supervisor or manager navigating the ideas and practices of feedback and other important topics. Or you could be a seasoned manager or restaurant owner finding ways to inspire your team. Use the book as a reference as you grow in your roles. I've also included a quick, "Into Action" section in the back with some other ways to use this book.

PART 1

1

Counter Styles

❦

Fast Food, Coffee Shops, Fast Casual

Fast Food

When we talk of fast food, most of us know what that means: McDonald's, Jack in the Box, Burger King, Taco Bell, etc. There are national chains, regional chains, and mom-and-pop versions of these types of restaurants everywhere. Hard to miss these as you drive down any highway or freeway. These restaurants usually have five to fifteen menu items, and if you work here your tasks are usually limited and repetitive. You may work as a cashier at the counter or a cashier at the drive-thru. Or you could be putting food that has already been assembled by the cooks onto a tray or into a to-go bag.

Coffee Shops

There are a wide range of coffee shops that serve many types of drinks and an assortment of food options. Starbucks and Peet's are a couple of national coffee chains, but there are amazing smaller chains and many owner-operated coffee shops all over our country. Each of these is delivering unique coffee, roasted many ways, and consistently improving their service to attract more guests. Some only sell products that have been delivered from a third-party kitchen (that is, someone else provides cold pastries, sandwiches, and desserts). Others will step it up a level and reheat food items that have already been prepared or par-cooked (breakfast sandwiches, panini, and warm desserts). Others may have a small prep area including high-end electric hot plates behind the counter and will make more complex dishes in-house. In any of these places, you may work behind the counter as a cashier or barista, or create meals by reheating, assembling orders, or cooking meals.

Fast Casual

Fast casual is a counter-style type of restaurant that you may be familiar with. At a typical fast-casual restaurant, the setup will be one of these:

- **You order at the counter, you pick your ingredients, they make your meal in front of you as you walk down the line, and they hand you your food right at the counter.**

- **You order at the counter, and you're given a number. Your order is brought to you at your table. Often cafés will offer this style of service, so those cafés could be considered fast casual.**

The current fast-casual restaurant movement, also referred to as QSR (quick-service restaurant), has many different styles of restaurants in varying levels of quality, offering many different types of cuisine, from quick assembled meals to intricately prepared meals. You could have something as streamlined as Chipotle or a restaurant with a detailed menu of fifteen items that are made fresh - with precision, detail, and modifications. It's an amazing time for restaurateurs, cooks, and counter servers who are looking to work in a fast-paced atmosphere while learning more about detailed quality food and beverage offerings.

Restaurants are switching out the Malibu chicken for the sous vide short rib sandwich, the Cobb salad for the Fattoush chicken salad, and the bear claw for cashew cream cheese toast with avocado. The structure of delivery has stayed somewhat the same in counter service, but ingredients have greatly improved. Standards are evolving quickly because guests' expectations are evolving just as quickly. The difference between fast food and fast casual is higher-quality food and higher prices, leading to higher wages and hopefully an elevated level of informed and gracious service.

Chefs from Tom Colicchio to Gordon Ramsey are opening high-end fast-casual restaurants everywhere. This makes sense because it is a different way of doing food than the intense, high-demand, labor-intensive ways that their flagship restaurants demand. In this scenario, they can make great food relatively quickly, with quality ingredients, and deliver it to the guest in an expedited manner. It's an amazing time to be a diner with all these types of restaurants in operation.

So, what does fast casual mean to the counter server or cashier? It means you must "up your game." You, in that position, need to know everything a traditional server would know about food and beverage. It's a leap from just smiling, greeting a guest, taking an order, and charging the guest. Now you must know the menu on a deeper level: know the specific ingredients, know where they come from, and be aware of the allergies that some dishes may aggravate. You are the direct connection to the kitchen. Your pace is much faster, because with a more intricate menu, your customers are going to ask more questions, want more details, and expect you to be a part of that dining experience. You are offering advice, taking the order, making the drinks, and processing their payment. You are creating a dining experience from the counter to the table.

Possible Positions

There are a few fast casual/ quick service restaurant models. They are ever-changing as restaurateurs are constantly coming up with ideas to best serve guests. The innovation that's happening with creative owners and chefs is fantastic! But it requires you, as a counter server, to adjust and improvise. You may work at a very streamlined restaurant that only has three or four main protein options with a few available toppings (e.g., Poke Palace, Chipotle). Or you may work in an upscale fast-casual restaurant where you need to know fifteen menu items and all the ingredients that go into them (some well-known national chains include Tender Greens, Blaze Pizza, and Panera). Regardless, here is a more detailed breakdown of the main positions you may find yourself working:

Sending order to kitchen, making drinks, cashier: The simplest layout is that you, the cashier, will help the guest by explaining the menu to them, taking their order, answering questions, and ringing them up. You charge them and give them their drink and a number that is on either a ticket or a stand. You could also be giving the guest a device that can alert the runner to deliver food to their table when it lights up, notifying the runner of the guest's location in the restaurant. The guests will take that number or device and find a seat at a table, and you or a teammate will bring their order to them once it is finished being prepared by the kitchen.

Serving prepared foods, making drinks, server: Some of the quicker fast casual places will have the menu items already prepared and in front of the guest, like a buffet, except the server is the only person with access to the food. The guest will move along in the line, as you ask them what they would like. You will be explaining the dishes and then putting the proper amount in their bowl, plate, or to-go container. And you or your co-worker will ring them up at the end of the line.

Preparing the dish itself, making drinks, cashier: Your third option is that you assemble the dish itself. This is where you, the server, will do all the above and build the dish for the guest: a burrito, taco, poke bowl, gyro, etc. The ingredients are there in front of you and you add them to the dish at the guest's request. You build their meal for them! By the end of the line, you get them something to drink and charge them, and they are on their way.

The Kitchen

Food can either be delivered and stored or made from scratch on site. Most food will be stored in the kitchen in large refrigerators (walk-ins). There are many types of fast casual restaurants: the simplest will have prepared foods delivered; the mid-size restaurant will make some of it on site; the higher-end culinary restaurants will make everything right there in a full on-site kitchen.

2

A GREAT JOB

---❖---

THE SWISS, SCHOOL GIGS, AND SIDE HUSTLES

You might be wondering why you would want a job in hospitality. In my years in the industry, I've had the opportunity to meet and work with people from all walks of life. People who work in these jobs are all ages and backgrounds, working to pay their bills, and some have a variety of other pursuits as well. In counter service, I've met people who are students, artists, entrepreneurs, and older employees looking to supplement their retirement benefits. There is a reason there is a wide variety of people coming together to take care of guests while making a living. No matter where you are in life, a job in hospitality can help you pursue your goals.

The Swiss

When I was sixteen, I quit working at our family lumberyard and got a dishwashing job on weekends at Mary's Pizza Shack. I lasted about three months. Cutting a bucket of tripe and a bucket of onions every night quickly took its smelly toll. I thankfully found a replacement job as a busboy at The Swiss. The Swiss Hotel was a small hotel, six rooms upstairs with a restaurant and bar downstairs. I had been going to The Swiss for dinner my whole life. I grew up knowing everyone who worked there. It was a small town. We celebrated a lot of the Farrell family birthdays at The Swiss every year.

I was a typical teenager, easily annoyed by my parents, and a job far away from them sounded good. Looking back, I was kind of a pain in the butt. Anything my parents told me to do, I had an amazing answer for why that was a bad idea. I think that's why my mom thought my working at The Swiss was the greatest idea on earth. I'd have to answer to Helen, and my smart mouth would either get me fired right away or get me a very stern and direct talking-to. It was the second option that worked.

Helen Dunlap was a great owner and bartender. She saw everything and was seamless in her service. She knew how to greet a family, hug a kid, remember a birthday, and direct an unruly drunk at the bar. I had known Helen my whole life. She was nice, but very direct. At the Swiss, the expectations were firm, and I wasn't allowed to goof off much. I could show my personality, but I had to do my job, or the other servers and Helen would intervene. In the dining room itself, I was coached by the three female servers. I used to joke that I now had five moms: one at home and four at The Swiss.

I learned so much more than how to bus tables. I learned about people. In the back of the house, there was a cast of oddball characters. In the front, I was exposed to many types of different people. Sonoma is a small town, but it is a big tourist destination. We were only an hour away from one of the busiest airports in the world. The Swiss hosted an eclectic mix of travelers and loyal locals. It was a great place to learn and a great place to be exposed to people from different places.

My boss and co-workers kept me in line and taught me a lot. I learned how to address people and pay attention: how to bring a good attitude to work, say good evening and goodbye, make eye contact, pay attention to details (if waters went unfilled, I heard about it), reset a table correctly. I learned about cleaning menus before service, folding napkins properly, and making sure I arrived to work with a clean uniform (yep, I got sent home a couple of times with a dirty shirt!) All things that I now know are Restaurant 101, I was introduced to by these awesome servers who took me under their wing as a high-school busboy.

LOOKING TO HELP OTHERS AND WORKING WITH A TEAM OF OTHER VOLUNTEERS, HAD A BIG IMPACT ON MY PERSONAL DEVELOPMENT AND HELPED ME EASILY TRANSITION INTO BEING OF SERVICE IN HOSPITALITY.

My uniform was black pants and a crisp white shirt with a bowtie. Yes, a bowtie! It was a clip-on, of course, because I had no idea how to tie a bowtie. (Honestly, I still don't.) I loved that uniform. I was excited that I got to wear a bowtie to work in an old Italian restaurant with checkered tablecloths. It made me feel like I mattered. I had a lot of pride when I would head off to work. It was a feeling I remember vividly. My mom still has a picture of me standing next to my ten-speed bicycle, in my uniform, ready to ride to work, with crisp shirt, bowtie, and a mouth full of shiny braces!

I became more confident in other areas of my life, while I learned all these things at The Swiss: how to listen, use conversation-starting questions, take direction, and engage with people while using the principles of good behavior. It was like a crash course in caring for people. My life really started to shift at this point. I was starting to learn a lot more than what was just inside my bedroom and the four walls of the Farrell house. This job made me focus less on me, brought me out of my head, and taught me some of my first lessons on what it means to be of service. It was my first introduction to a job where we made money caring for people, while working with a team to provide a great way for people to enjoy themselves.

I grew up in a home where volunteering was just part of what we did. In a small town it seemed like everybody was always helping people. My siblings and I helped my parents at church, the Community Center, and volunteering at other places. Our town had many clubs and groups that helped people: Kiwanis and Lions clubs, different church and social groups, nonprofits, free or low-cost kids' sports leagues, all providing community outreach that focused on helping people and creating a great, accessible town to live in. The culture of volunteering, looking to help others and working with a team of other volunteers, had a big impact on my personal development and helped me easily transition into being of service in hospitality and getting my job at The Swiss.

School Gig

You could be in high school working a few hours after school or only on the weekend. Maybe you are in college, taking twelve units a semester and needing to make some dough on the side. You may be living with your family, chipping in on bills, or living on your own. Or you are working to gain experience for your résumé, learn skills, and earn some spending money. Or you are paying for college and/or making up what your student loans don't cover. You could be searching for a job that can cover your health benefits while you pursue your education.

Hospitality jobs can be flexible, easy to find, and dependable. They are flexible because many places have night shifts for people going to school during the day and day shifts for those who prefer classes at night. Some counter-service jobs can fit students in on the weekend if they cannot work during the week because of school commitments. Not to mention early-morning coffee shifts that allow you to make it to your 10 a.m. history class. These are dependable jobs, and this type of work experience makes you a frontrunner for other jobs when you move towns or schools or want to move up in the hospitality industry.

A lot of part-time seasonal jobs involve working retail, data entry, lifeguarding, babysitting, or tutoring, but these counter-service jobs I'm talking about can help you make money year-round and even give you job options after you have your diploma in your hand. This certainly doesn't limit you to just food and beverage establishments. What I learned the most when I worked in counter service in college was about dealing with people, reading guests, and improving my interpersonal skills. This made me easily hirable in other areas and industries that wanted someone who had experience with customer service and front-facing guests.

HAVING A HISTORY OF WORKING WITH TEAMS, TAKING DIRECTION, AND LEARNING THE FUNDAMENTALS OF CUSTOMER SERVICE WILL ONLY BENEFIT YOU AS YOU MOVE ON FROM SCHOOL IN PURSUIT OF OTHER DREAMS.

You have to find the job that's right for you. So, think about your neighborhood, hometown, or college area for a moment. What are the types of counter service jobs that come to mind? There are lots of coffee shops, fast food, and fast casual places. All of these can offer shifts at varying points in the day to offset your school schedule. Scout the places that you might like to work. If you can't afford a full meal, go in for a coffee, soda, or dessert. Something that won't break the bank but will give you an idea of the style and type of place it is. See if you can imagine yourself working there. You want to find a place you *want* to work.

As you go to school, you may stay at the same job or move on to other types of jobs in more complex restaurants. Some counter-style spots also are great stepping-stones into roles in full-service restaurants. Hosts and hostesses are often hired if they have had some counter service experience. A full-service restaurant is more likely to give someone a chance at being a server if they have had time to interact with different types of guests in a counter-service atmosphere. They want to know you have some experience and can overcome challenges with guests. My friend Alice started at a Subway in her first year of college. Midway through college she was a server at Chili's, and by senior year was working as a bartender to help pay her tuition.

Time in any of these jobs is fantastic work experience for any opportunity you may be pursuing after school. Almost all businesses want someone who has work experience. And this type of work provides you with the experience of dealing with different types of guests, needs, and interactions. You will have stories you can tell in your interviews about winning over a guest, improving your communication skills, and learning how to pay attention to details while multitasking.

Having a history of working with teams, taking direction, and learning the fundamentals of customer service will only benefit you as you move on from school in pursuit of other dreams. You will be better prepared to interact with future fellow employees, managers, and leadership. A counter service job is a great way to get an on-the-job education while you are learning and pursuing your institutional education.

The Side Hustle

While most people are working full-time in counter service jobs, some are just looking to work part-time. This may be because they have another job and are looking to add hours and pay to that main job, trying to make extra money to help them pay their bills, or even have their own businesses but need extra income or insurance.

Most of my artist friends have had side jobs that help them pay their rent and bills. Some of these jobs turn into their main means of income. Most of my friends enjoy the opportunity to be in a job where they get to interact with people, since their artistic work can be somewhat isolating. Counter service jobs are a great way to make money and create a work/life balance that fits you.

Counter service jobs in hospitality are a great source of income for retirees who are looking to increase their income to supplement their retirement benefits. Many people who have retired from their "career" job look forward to a job in hospitality where they can work fewer hours, make money, and interact with a variety of guests and co-workers.

3

BEING PREPARED

POLITE, ON TIME, AND PRESENTABLE

These three points don't waver in any job. They are the basis for the agreement that you make with your employer when they hire you. In this type of work, a successful business depends on an employee being able to, at the very least, show up with a good attitude, at the time the company needs them, dressed in clean, proper clothing. If you want to do well in your job, these are three of the most basic commitments you need to remember to follow.

Polite

My mom used to tell my brother and me, "It doesn't cost you anything to be polite." I'm consistently surprised that politeness is the key ingredient missing from most service interactions. Think about your daily experiences at the grocery store, the bank, the deli, the convenience store, the school office, the gas station. The list goes on. See if the counter person engages you first. If they say hello or hi and make eye contact with you. In the last couple of weeks alone, I've had these situations occur:

- **Cashier at the local gas station who didn't even make eye contact with me, just said, "What pump?" and took my money. End of transaction.**

- Cashier at our local grocery store who faked a smile, rang up our groceries, told me (not asked) to punch in my rewards number and barely managed an unenthusiastic, "Bye."

- Cashier at a local coffee spot who, when I said, "Good morning, how are you?" answered, "Tired. What are you having?" They took my order, flipped the iPad around on the swivel showing me the tip page with 20 percent, 25 percent, 30 percent, and nodded to no one in particular, after I swiped my card. Then moved over to the machine, made my coffee, yelled over the machine at a co-worker, and called out my name like there were twenty people in the place (there were four) and pushed my coffee off onto a waiting table, neither making eye contact nor mustering a "goodbye."

You may be thinking, "Dude, you should move out of your neighborhood!" But interactions like these are common everywhere.

The definition of *polite* that I heard growing up was something like this: "Having or showing behavior that is respectful and considerate of other people." Hospitality and food service is not "I'll stay in my lane, you stay in yours." Or "I'm being considerate of you by minding my own business." Hospitality is different. In hospitality, politeness requires action. It requires us to reach out to our guests first, not to wait for them to come to us.

We give that respect to our guests by being proactive and showing them consideration. We don't wait for them to earn our respect; we automatically give it to them. That's the deal. Regardless of who they are, what they look like, or the type of the day they are having, we give our customers and guests respect because they have chosen to come into our business and do business with us. They chose us, today, over our competition. So, they earn that respect by just walking through our door. And our job is to give it to them.

We show our respect by turning our attention to them, engaging with them as soon as we see them enter our business. Make eye contact with them and be present. A nod of the head, a smile at least. We show politeness and respect in many other ways as well:

- **We choose to think of them as a guest instead of a customer. This puts us in a mode of extra care.**

- **We give them our attention with a smile when they walk into our store or approach us.**

- **We smile at our guest when they are within ten feet of us or say hi and verbally acknowledge them when they are within five feet of us.**

- **We thank our guests when they purchase something from us. And we wish them a good day.**

This is the job. The job isn't "Sit here all day, don't make eye contact, don't say hi, ring them up, take their payment, and look as bored as possible." That isn't what people are for. If that's the role you are looking for, there are plenty of options outside of hospitality, food, and beverage. Engaging with a guest in a polite way isn't extra. It's not a favor. These actions of politeness are not outside of the customer-service job description. They *are* customer service.

If you can connect with the customer in a friendly way that ensures they have a good enough moment that they choose to come back to the business, then that is a win. That's it. So, who cares if it's a restaurant, café, grocery store, or Bob's Boring Service Center? Politeness is a two-to-five-second adjustment that can happen anywhere—an instant contrast with the miserable interactions that already happen at other counters.

The good news is, in food and beverage, this is what we call hospitality, and we have been doing this type of great service for years. This is a tradition in our counter service culture. We engage. We ask questions. We provide service with a smile. When we don't do this, we give people a reason to walk down the street and spend their money in a different coffee shop, cafe, or restaurant. Customers routinely come back to companies that have good service, polite service...even if their product is a little more expensive than a similar company that has horrible service. Service matters. Politeness matters. And it doesn't cost you anything.

Time

One of the elements that comes up a lot in hospitality is the concept of time. There are many expectations that involve time: your responsibilities to the company you work for and the company's commitment to its guests.

Before I worked in restaurants, I had a pretty lax view of time. When I worked for my dad, I realized he didn't mind if a was a couple of minutes late. That was not the case once I started working for non-family at Mary's Pizza Shack and The Swiss. These people knew how to run restaurants, they had been doing it a long time, and when I showed up late, I heard about it, loud and clear. There was no tolerance for being late.

This is the commitment and contract you make when you are hired. It doesn't matter if it's a well-known coffee chain or your friend's parents' deli. You show up, *ready to work* at the start of your scheduled shift. There will be moments when you are late for valid reasons, but they should be very rare. Let me be clear. It doesn't mean you run into the back of the restaurant and clock in as the clock hits 5:00—then take your time getting ready for your shift, use the restroom, spruce up your hair, and arrive behind the counter at 5:09. Don't be the person who is always late. It's not cool. Even if co-workers say they don't mind, they do. Respect their time by honoring yours.

There are many policies about calling out of work. The main one is: if you aren't feeling well, you shouldn't come to work. You should stay home and get better and come back healthy. Most companies have a policy that says you must call out of your shift a few hours before your shift starts—no last-minute call-offs. This is so they can prepare for your absence. As a server, I used to work in some family owned, smaller-staff restaurants, so if I couldn't cover my shift, and I really wasn't feeling well, I'd call as early as I could. All of us who worked there tried to follow this unwritten rule. We wanted to give the team time to adjust. Your absence can really affect the workload of everyone you work with—always be aware of that. It's best to give everyone a chance to fill your position, so they aren't short-staffed, your absence doesn't overwhelm your co-workers, and the place provides seamless service for the guests.

THE MORE YOU PAY ATTENTION TO HONORING YOUR TIME MANAGEMENT, THE FASTER THOSE SKILLS WILL GROW, AND IT WILL IMMEDIATELY IMPROVE YOUR RELATIONSHIPS WITH YOUR CO-WORKERS, BOSSES, AND THE GUESTS.

I was working at a hotel in downtown LA, and the front desk manager had us do this exercise during Line-up. (Line-up is a pre-shift meeting that occurs in restaurants and hotels.) In this exercise, the manager had us pick a spot on the ceiling and just stare at it in silence. He told us he would tell us when to stop. It seemed like it took five minutes. When he said, "Finished," we all looked around at each other. He asked us how long it had been. Most of us guessed between three and five minutes. It had been one minute. We always lose track of time. When we tell someone "a few minutes," a few minutes to me is different than a few minutes to you. It leaves a lot of room for error or misinterpretation, and those are never good in hospitality. When a guest asks you how long something is going to take, really give them an honest answer. Try to be as specific as possible. When people are waiting for a long time, they have more time to make up ideas of how you could do your job more efficiently, so don't give them that extra time.

Almost all fast-casual restaurants I've been to are order-fire restaurants (that means when the cashier presses Send on the ticket, it goes to the kitchen and the cooks start cooking). It's important to know that when there is a big wait, you should be aware of how long a product may take to prepare. If only four people just went through the line and ordered the same thing, the time to prepare it may only be eight minutes. If you are slammed and twelve people just went through the line and ordered the same thing, the order may take longer, fifteen minutes. You will understand these as you adjust to the style of your restaurant. For a great guest experience, always give them as accurate a time as possible.

"I'll be back in five," is what my co-worker Sheryl would say. And we would all kind of giggle. Sheryl was never back in five. Usually, fifteen minutes. Sheryl had been at this restaurant longer than most of the servers but was not our manager or supervisor. "Can you cover my section? Be back in five." "Sure, Sheryl." It didn't take long for resentment to build. It could start to seem like Sheryl was taking advantage of us or thought we didn't know how to read a clock. Don't be like Sheryl. Take your break and take the exact time you tell people you are going to. We all know how to tell time; we all have clocks on us. It doesn't fool anyone when you are later than you said you would be. It just opens the possibility that co-workers think you are taking advantage of them, and that can build resentment, and that's not good for teamwork.

These aspects of time management are important when you are working with a team and serving guests. Many issues always arise around time. The more you pay attention to honoring your time management, the faster those skills will grow, and it will immediately improve your relationships with your co-workers, bosses, and the guests.

Front Lawns and Barbers

When I was a kid, my brother and I would mow the lawn as part of our chores. My dad brought home a manual edger one day. I had no idea what it was used for. It looked like a weapon from *Game of Thrones*. It was a sharp device on a wheel that was connected to a handle, like a broom or rake. As an eleven-year-old,

I was not happy with another step in the chore process. I was sure this edging business would eat into my play time. But I watched my dad use it and it seemed pretty quick. He took the sharp device and rolled it along where the lawn met the pavement. It cut any grass that was splayed out over the edge of the pavement.

I'm not saying I wanted to *do* it, but I saw its payoff immediately. It made the lawn look so much better. It was tight. The grass was already cut, but now it had a clean border that made the lawn look super-sharp. It had a beautiful frame. We started using this edger on yards my brother and I cut in the neighborhood, and I truly think that this edger alone got us more work from other neighbors. People loved our lawns.

KEEP YOUR CASHIER AREA CLEAN, YOUR ESPRESSO STATION ORGANIZED, THE TABLES ALIGNED, THE CHAIRS MATCHING EACH OTHER AT EACH TABLE.

Many, many years later, I was staying with my friend Tim in Flatbush, Brooklyn. I had my head shaved at the time, and it being the middle of summer, hot and humid, it was a good style to have. The close cut was new to me, and it required hitting up the local barbershop more frequently. I found a place in Tim's neighborhood and walked in, asked for a cut, and sat down. I was thinking that it would take five minutes. That's how long it had taken my last guy at a barbershop on Broadway in Lower Manhattan. Three on top, two on the side, a quick blend, and I was out of there. But it took this guy in Brooklyn thirty-five minutes to shave my head.

He took his time on the blend, the fade, and the details of the lines around the cut. Precision. The hairline meeting the forehead, around the ears and down the side of the neck to the back of the neck, the line across the back of my head, and up and around the other side. At times his stern and focused face was a foot from mine. He switched up clippers several times: calm hand, moving slow and very deliberately. And he didn't say a word. There was no chitchat. This guy was taking care of business.

I was thinking, "Wow. This is taking incredibly long," but a twelve-dollar haircut is a good deal, so I let the man do his thing.

When I got home, I stared in the mirror at that buzzcut. *Dang, this is the tightest, best haircut I have ever received!* And I got a lot of compliments—on a shaved head!

I've often thought of that lawn edger and haircut throughout my life. Unexpectedly, I was reminded of them when I got into restaurant work. I was taught that in service, alignment matters! Just like a tight haircut, matching your eye makeup on your left and right eyes, or taking time to keep your shoes looking fresh and clean—all of us already have experience with symmetry and organization. You already have a sense of the impact.

In our work environment, we need to magnify this idea. That's how we let guests know we are prepared for them. We care about them. That's why you keep your cashier area clean, your espresso station organized, the tables aligned, the chairs matching each other at each table. It's why we pay attention when we roll our utensils the correct way every time and why we place that coffee or drink in front of a guest with the company logo on the cup or glass always facing the guest.

This translates to how you present yourself in a clean uniform—or if you don't have a uniform, a clean outfit. I've been in some hipster, casual cafés, where their intent is to give off a loose, bohemian vibe. But the successful ones are able to do that while maintaining great service, attention to detail, and cleanliness.

Every detail makes a big difference. And like edging a lawn, it takes less time than you think. I know, creating symmetry and order in your station may feel stiff at first, but the more you do it, the more it becomes second nature. When you do, you will convey to the guest that you are taking care of them. You are paying attention. That's what makes you a service professional.

4

HIRED

AN OVER-VIEW OF WHAT TO EXPECT

Day 1

Every company is going to be different, but here are a few points you should have prepared for your first day of work. Pay attention to any email or phone conversation you have prior to arriving on your first day. It's important that you clearly understand and write down whatever directions they give you. You will want to bring all the items they request. Here are a few things to think about:

- **Plan to arrive on time.**

  - **Check your commute time via bike, car, or public transportation**

  - **Your commute time may be different depending on the day of week, time of day, or traffic**

  - **I like to arrive ten minutes before to ensure I'm ready**

- **Dress similar to how you dressed for your interview, unless instructed otherwise.**

- **Know your uniform sizes: shirt size, pants size, hat size.**

- **Bring your Employment Eligibility Verification, needed in most cases.**

  - A state or government issued ID card or passport

  - A current state license

  - A Social Security card and/or birth certificate

- **If applicable, bring a current state food handler certificate.**

- **Ensure your IDs and certificates are up-to-date and NOT expired.**

- **Bring bank information: Your account numbers to sign up for direct deposit, if it's an option that is more convenient for you.**

- **Bring a simple notepad or notebook with a pen. You will be getting a lot of information on your first day, so come prepared.**

- **Wear comfortable shoes and if applicable, a hair tie.**

- **Pack lunch or dinner: I wouldn't assume there is a company meal provided.**

- **Put your phone on silent before you walk in the door.**

Training

Once you are hired, you should get a description of all the menu items they expect you to know. Get on it. Flashcards, phone recorders, whatever. Start now.

Training will depend on the restaurant and the management. Most of the time, you will get computer training and food and beverage training. This will be during service with staff and could be done via computer tutorials as well. The expectations at most places are the same. Learn it fast and well so they can get you up to speed quickly. Training can take two weeks, so be prepared and focused.

Computer

Most items in a restaurant are entered/ordered into a computer system call a POS—a Point of Sale system. There are large systems such as Micros, Aloha, and Squirl. A POS system can also operate through a tablet, phone, or other mobile device. Square, Clover, and Toast are a few I've seen using these devices. This type of POS is a little more movable, often on a swivel, and allows the customers to swipe a card, add a tip, or provide a signature. In counter service, you may have a few types of ordering situations using one of these:

- **An order that you type in and is relayed to the kitchen so it can be prepared.**

- **An order that you type in and is relayed to the barista to prepare.**

- **An order that you type in and prepare or assemble yourself or with a co-worker.**

Line-Up

Sometimes referred to as *stand-up*—not to be confused with time to jump on the comedy stage—this is a pre-shift meeting lasting anywhere from three to ten minutes. Unfortunately, many times line-ups are skipped in more casual restaurants because there is no official closing of the restaurant, and somebody is always watching the counter or the floor. Line-up is a time to focus for the shift and cross-check some information. It usually involves the staff, manager, and chef, but can include just two people.

Information discussed may include:

- **Position assignments for the shift if not previously assigned**

- **Items that the restaurant has run out of that may still exist on the menu/menu board**

- **Any items that have a low count (meaning only a few more exist and will most likely run out during the shift)**

- **Any items that are substituting certain ingredients in place of ones that have run out**

- **New menu items and their descriptions**

- **Picking some specific points of service to focus on during this shift**

- **Selecting sales goals for the shift and sharing selling tactics**

- **Sharing positive notes or feedback with the team**

- **Sharing constructive feedback from guests or ownership with the team**

- **If any equipment is out of service that will affect the team and guests**

- **If short-staffed, how the team will manage with one less member for the shift**

As you can see, a lot of information can be discussed in a short time frame. This is a moment to focus for your shift and ask any questions you may need clarification for. This is a good time to switch gears and put yourself in the mode of serving guests. If you don't have a line-up where you work, you still need to answer some of these questions for yourself—especially menu items that have run out or have not been changed on the menu or board. This is part of being prepared to serve your guests. You never want to tell a guest how great an item is, only to then look down and realize you are out of it. It makes you look like you don't know how to do your job.

Allergies

It's very important that you pay attention to what common allergies may be affected by certain dishes. Listen to guests and relay any specific allergies to the chef, cooks, or relevant co-workers. You don't want to make mistakes with allergies. Always put it in the computer for each dish the guest orders. If you are using a handwritten system, ensure it is clearly written so the kitchen can read the warning. A very caring touch is to restate the allergen to the guest when you deliver their food. "Here is your Spring Salad with no walnuts." When it comes to coffee, it's a nice touch to reassure that it's decaf if that's what they ordered. Some guests will have an allergic reaction to caffeine.

ALWAYS REPEAT THE ORDER TO YOUR GUESTS, AND ALWAYS DOUBLE-CHECK BEFORE YOU HIT SEND.

Money

You eventually will be working on the register. Anything that has to do with money and payment needs your focus. The entire operation hinges on this. You should receive extensive training about working on the register and cash-handling policies. If you don't know something or an issue arises that you are unsure of, *ask someone!* Ask immediately; not "when I have a second." I've seen people start fiddling around with buttons—they hit the wrong one and erase four hours of payments. Most companies know the importance of training in this area but keep your attention on all things about the register and payments. Don't get cocky and don't be shy about asking for help if you are unsure.

Taking the Order

An important aspect of working the line as cashier/server is that you also need to be aware of the back of house. (Traditionally, in sit-down full-service restaurants, *back of house* refers to anyone who works in the kitchen and *front of house* refers to all of the people who are working directly with the guests, for example: cashiers, hosts, servers, runners, bussers.) Most counter-service-style restaurants don't take reservations, so there is no way to determine how many guests will come in at any given time. You are the first person to engage with the guest and will see if the restaurant is about to get slammed. You will get used to the firing times and have a general idea of how long it takes the kitchen at certain busy parts of the shift. Be aware and communicate with your co-workers and manager so you can be successful in getting guests their meals in a timely manner. Remember, it's a team effort. You want to take care of the kitchen, ensure they aren't swamped, and learn about pacing the line. By working together, everyone will succeed.

FOOD ALLERGIES INCREASE AS INGREDIENTS INCREASE.
KNOW YOUR MENU WELL, LISTEN CAREFULLY,
DOUBLE-CHECK WITH THE GUEST.

Details of the Order

Putting the order in correctly is very important. This is to ensure a steady flow of service, make sure the kitchen has the exact order, and guarantee any modifications by the guest are communicated correctly. Modifications occur for many reasons. Food allergies increase as ingredients increase. Know your menu well, listen carefully, double-check with the guest, and make sure the information makes its way into the computer correctly. You are the face of the restaurant and need to remain calm and gracious no matter how busy the line gets. You will get used to the pace and speed at which the restaurant works best. Don't get too overwhelmed when you start a new position. If you find yourself getting overwhelmed with your job you can always move ahead in the book and look at the chapter titled The Reset.

Double-Check

Always repeat the order to your guests, and always double-check before you hit Send. This is something I've heard my whole life in restaurants. There is nothing more irritating to the kitchen or co-workers than starting to prepare a meal or drink to later find out that it was entered into the computer wrong. Mistakes happen, of course. But really make it a habit for every transaction you do on a computer. Always clarify the order with your guests, and always double-check before you push Enter or Send. If you are working a drive-thru or to-go pickup counter, always repeat the order before handing it to the guest.

Delivering Food to the Table

If the customer gets a number for their order at your restaurant, then you or a co-worker will be delivering food to their table. In general, in this situation, you want to make sure of three things:

- **Each plate has the correct items on it.**

- **All the food items for the number are ready. This is so you don't deliver food to the table and keep one person waiting an extra five to ten minutes because of a kitchen issue. Having everyone eating at the table while one person waits never turns out to be a good online review!**

- **When you drop off the dish, you want to announce it. A general rule is to say the name of the dish, and one or two main items in it. E.g., "Here is your Moroccan salad with steak," or "This is our grilled salmon with asparagus." You want to do this for**

three reasons: It's a great way to present the restaurant's food by defining the dishes you are putting down, you want to ensure that each person is getting the dish they ordered, and it gives you an opportunity to ask if you may bring anything else for them.

Do a Lap

Always walk back through the dining room and see how your guests are enjoying their food and/or drinks. I call it doing a lap. It's vital to good service. If someone needs something—a condiment, napkin, a refill—you have a chance to do that for them before it's too late. You have an opportunity to fix an issue if anyone has a problem with their drink or dish. So, try to check in with the table a couple of minutes after they sit down with their food, or it's delivered to the table. Ask them how they are enjoying their coffee/pastry/meal. This is a point of service that shows your guests you care about their experience.

Side Work

"Jimmy didn't do his side work again!" Don't be Jimmy! Every job you have in a restaurant will have side work associated with it. Rolling silverware, refilling condiments, refilling napkins, replacing utensils, cleaning restrooms, ensuring tables aren't wobbly, etc. The list can be longer depending on the complexity of the operation. Don't leave your side work for someone else to do! There is always someone who just does the bare minimum. It creates a lot of resentment in co-workers. And if you think they don't notice, you are wrong. This has happened in every restaurant I've ever worked in. You can always tell yourself, "There are enough sugars in the container, enough soap in the dispenser, enough napkins in the holder." That's not the question. The question is, is it full? Does it look full and ready for a guest? Don't cut corners and leave more work for the next person. If you complete your side work fully and quickly, your team will appreciate you.

Downtime

My friend Gio had a sign in his restaurant, "What to do when there is nothing to do." There was a list below it that had a variety of tasks, "Fold Boxes, check to-go supplies, study menu ingredients, etc." It's important to be able to accomplish some tasks while you are waiting for guests to come up to the counter. It beats looking bored as heck or staring off into space as you stand at the register. An issue that can arise from this multi-tasking, is you can get caught up in the task and forget the primary purpose, which is the guest experience. When a guest is in the area or approaching, you want to stop doing your task, your side work, and give your complete attention to the guest. While you may enjoy talking with a co-worker as you accomplish side work, always make sure you are scanning the counter and keeping your priority on guests.

Cleanliness

Dirty tables should be cleaned quickly and efficiently, while not making a lot of noise. It never looks good for a table to be dirty for longer than a few minutes after it has been vacated by guests. Sometimes the guests will clear their table, but when they don't, attending to the table and cleaning it should be done quickly and thoroughly, so other guests may use it. If silverware or plate ware has been used, be careful not to make too much noise with clanking, so as not to disturb the diners still eating in the restaurant.

We are looking out for safety our guests and each other. Given the last few years of a pandemic, we want our guests to know that we always maintain a primary focus on cleanliness. Restaurants have always had this priority in regard to food safety, but it's now very magnified, and the expectations are even higher from guests. Ensure you wash your hands regularly, wear PPE when appropriate, and try to maintain a clean workplace. Some businesses have "open kitchens," which means our guests can see us as we make and assemble food. I address cleanliness more in the section titled Safety.

5

SIZZLER

THE ORIGINAL FAST-CASUAL

I started serving tables in between my first and second years of college. A girl who was a few years ahead of me mentioned that she was making pretty good money working at a restaurant near the school. I was nineteen at the time, and I needed a side gig while I was in school. I worked at Sizzler three or four nights a week for the next three years.

When the current fast casual/QSR movement started to increase I thought back to this college job I had. Sizzler was one of the original fast-casual places before the phrase even existed. The setup was similar in that guests would order at the counter, receive their drinks, and seat themselves in the restaurant. The server—me—would pick up the ticket, take it to the back, and put it in the pass (the window into the kitchen). When the order came up in the window that matched their ticket number, I would bring the food out to the table and announce it to the guests, and then bring any other items associated with their order.

Sizzler had a strict rule of checking back at the table within two minutes of the food being delivered. The only reason I remember this is I would get in trouble when I first started for not getting back to the table within that time frame. It was very clear then that the job isn't done when you give the food to the guest.

It was a very simple system. Sizzler also had a great salad bar, and guests could just purchase the salad bar or add it to their entrees. My job as the server was to ensure that the table was detailed: dirty plates were cleared, soft drinks and waters refilled, condiments brought, and any special requests taken care of. If a guest had ordered dessert, the servers, at the correct time, would put the finishing touches on a pre-made dessert and bring it out to the table.

THE JOB ISN'T DONE WHEN YOU GIVE THE FOOD TO THE GUEST.

In retrospect, what I think Sizzler excelled at was guaranteeing that the guest had a very good dining experience from ordering at the counter until walking out the door. Sizzler could have simply let people fend for themselves without a server. Guests liked that someone was consistently walking through, and checking in. Someone was paying attention to them, could take care of their needs, and cared about their experience. That's why people came back. The majority of our business was return customers.

For a college student, I thought it was the greatest job in the world. I was serving people from all walks of life. I had just moved to Los Angeles from a small town of 10,000 people. I got to work with a very cool group of people, all of whom were pursuing other things. A graduate student, a newly hired court stenographer who wasn't getting enough hours at the court yet, a single mom, a girl a few years older than me who was starting a jewelry business, a guy in his thirties who needed an extra few bucks to make his mortgage.

It was a great place to get my first job as a server. Sizzler had an easy-to-follow training system, company Steps of Service, tips on being positive, making eye contact and smiling. They ensured every guest had a great dining experience while in the restaurant.

6

EXCELLING IN YOUR JOB

CHALLENGING YOURSELF, KNOWING WHAT YOU SELL, AND USING PEOPLE'S NAMES

There are a few things that have helped me excel at my jobs early on in hospitality. I've always looked for ways to stay interested in the day-to-day duties as well as trying to stand out from employees who were just cruising by. You have to make decisions that will keep you inspired by your work. Challenging yourself everyday will keep you moving upward, and paying attention to details will make a huge difference with your managers and guests. Here are three key points that I've always focused on.

Challenge Yourself

Once you've gotten your job and gone through training, you have a choice to make. You can find the path of least resistance or you can make you job mean something to you. It can be hard to learn a new position or role and all the tasks that are associated with executing it. And often these roles can require self-motivation. I've always adhered to the notion that what you put into the job, you get out. It's why I think making your job mean something to you and having some sort of touchstone to get you through the day are so important. Whatever your goals and objectives are in your life (like paying your bills, pursuing your dreams, connecting with people), those things can align with your objectives and goals at your job. Hustling is a great attribute to have and one that will always turn heads at your job, but working smart is what brings that hustle into overdrive, makes you efficient, and moves you well beyond the rest.

Depending on the size of the operation, you will have a wide range of employees having mixed feelings about their job and the business. Some people will be happy to work at the business, some will be fine with it, some unhappy, and some outright miserable. I've seen the whole range, oftentimes under one roof. When you start off at a new job, you have a unique opportunity that can take you down one of two roads. You can align yourself with the unhappy, complaining crowd, or you can align yourself with the people who look like they enjoy working at this business. This will be a crossroads you will come to many times in your working life.

I'm not a "You must be Mister Happy Pants all the time" guy. Believe me. I've had my ups and downs. That is part of the job. You will feel all the things I mentioned above, and that is OK. That is part of the human experience and certainly part of the job experience. What I would like you to be aware of is there are some people you will work with who will choose to be unhappy in their work situation, rather than move on from it. If you're unhappy or complacent in your job, hopefully you can find something that makes work a little more interesting and enjoyable to you.

FIND SOMEONE WHO IS DOING THE JOB GREAT, EXCITED TO BE THERE, AND EXCELLING AT THE POSITION YOU HAVE OR WANT.

I worked with a guy, Michael, who, every time I asked him how his day was going, would reply, "Another day, another dollar." Michael was fine. He wasn't miserable. He did his job. He didn't enjoy engaging with people and he liked to be very focused on his own tasks. He didn't possess a lot of vision about what was going on around him. Michael was not the best candidate for a front-facing position and greeting guests, but here we were. You could tell he wasn't happy at his tables and was just there for his check. It was difficult to keep the team upbeat when he was there because he put a bit of a drag on service.

Hospitality is not an "another day, another dollar" job. It's just not. This job requires more of you than that, and it's important that you know this is part of the expectations from the get-go. When we are asked to engage with our guests, we need to bring a certain energy and feeling about our job to that experience every day, every time. Through good training, you can make a tough day a little brighter by connecting with others. You will always have a choice which group you want to surround yourself with.

So, pick your heroes carefully. When I used to play sports more often, I would always pick someone to play with who was 10–15 percent better than me to learn from. It made me play "up," or challenge myself to play better. I didn't want to get schooled on the court, but I didn't want to be bored either. I wanted to learn, to push myself a bit. You have a great opportunity when you start a job to pick your hero and follow them. The hero is not going to be "Another day, another dollar" Michael. It's not going to be the person who believes, "This place is awful, but that's just the way it is." Find someone who is doing the job great, excited to be there, and excelling at the position you have or want. Copy the employees who seem to be doing their job well, not cutting corners and whispering, "We aren't supposed to do it this way, but honestly, it's easier for me and the guests won't even know." Always pick the person you admire and think you can learn the most from. Always "play up."

Know What You Sell

I was at a restaurant recently with some friends, and our friend Liza asked our server how the salmon was prepared, and the server said, "Um. Well…it's cooked.

It comes with, um, vegetables, and I believe there is a lemon on the plate. I think it's a Meyer lemon." Not the world's best explanation of a dish. A little unsure with the *ums* and the "I believe" and "I think." It reminded me of a moment I had at a well-known coffee house many years ago when I asked what a macchiato was and the cashier said, after a slight pause, "I think it's like a latte, but smaller."

I'm not a stickler for much, but I do expect people to know the menu when I walk into their restaurant. That's the way our companies make money. The company sells a product. We are all salespeople who sell the product for the companies we work for. You don't want to be the server who is reading your own menu to the guest because you can't remember what's on it. So, if you don't know what you're selling, what are you doing here? You have to know what your company sells. In detail. That is a large part of your job.

If you were buying a car from me, and you asked me if the car has four-wheel drive, and I said, "I think it does," you'd probably say, "Well, does it or not?" And then I'd have to go check. You aren't going to feel very sure of me as I continue to tell you things about the car, right? You might even think I'm making stuff up. It simply doesn't look good to our guests when we stumble and don't know what the product is.

> YOU DON'T WANT TO BE THE SERVER WHO IS READING
> YOUR OWN MENU TO THE GUEST BECAUSE YOU CAN'T
> REMEMBER WHAT'S ON IT.

If you were buying a video game from me, and you asked, "Is this the one with the golden castles that I fly into on my Skyhawk?" and I said, "I think so," you'd probably look at me funny and think, "I'm not dropping my $40 on this until I'm sure it's the one I want." Maybe you would ask me to ask my boss or another associate who actually knew the product.

You don't always have to know every detail. Moments will happen when you don't, and it's always OK to tell your guest, "I don't know, but let me find that information out for you." It's a definitive answer. And you can step away and ask someone who has that information. Knowing what you are talking about is reassuring to the guest, and it leads to a trust between you and the guest. If you like a particular drink or food item and you can recommend that in detail to a guest and they like it, you can be sure they will ask your advice in the future. It's one of the ways we build relationships in hospitality.

A great server I've worked with—who crushed wine sales—was my friend Jason. We worked at an intimate restaurant in Santa Monica with a wine list that had over 3,000 wines on it. It was massive. I would come in and Jason would always be looking at the wine list for at least ten to fifteen minutes before each shift. He also had a folder that he kept in the back with his extensive wine notes. He'd jot stuff in this binder after looking up info on his phone or talking with one of the other servers who had some great talking points. He was great with guests and quick with an explanation: tell a guest why they would like the wine, a cool anecdote about it, and why it would pair well with what they were ordering.

Because of his studying, he had a confidence about him. And if he was unsure about a wine, he didn't hesitate to ask any of the other servers who had a stronger knowledge of a particular region of the world. Here's the thing: Jason didn't drink alcohol- since way before he had even stepped in a restaurant. What he did have was this thirst for knowledge and expertise at what we sold in our restaurant. He studied. He was prepared. And that allowed him to be friendly and easy at a table, while casually and confidently selling them a $300 bottle of wine. Repeatedly.

Menus will change, especially since guests now expect seasonal offerings and special featured items. As these new products are released, the expectations of your bosses are that you learn and remember what those items are. I used a little recorder for years to talk into and then listen to in my car or on the bus on my way to work. I would record new specials, descriptions of dishes, and new drinks. When I started at a new place, I would try to get pictures (or take them, if they allowed) because I tend to remember information faster if I have a picture to look at while I memorize. Flashcards have always been my go-to.

This is a book about service, the guest experience, and how we can make that better. But at the very base of what we do, we are salespeople who have to sell the product provided by our company. If you know your products well, you can upsell the experience to your guests, build great relationships, and keep them coming back.

Names

I've never been one of those people who have a great knack for remembering names. I've always been good with faces and stories. I can remember a person's face, favorite sports team, where they are from, the drink they always order. Everyone has their strengths in this area. My teacher from tenth grade, Mr. Morrish, knew every one of his students' names by day two. He got great pleasure telling us each desk where our brothers and sisters sat when they were in his class—eight years prior. We, of course, were in awe of this.

It makes sense that teachers are good at the name game, as their objective is to connect with their students as quickly as possible. I know I respond well to people who remember my name. It makes me feel more comfortable, immediately creates a familiar sense, and connects me to that person. Using the other person's name naturally is one of the most important elements of interaction in hospitality. Using the guest's name makes them feel engaged and unique, not just a random person lost in a sea of others.

Often guests will give you their name when you request it for their order. Happens in a coffee shop all the time. Not only is it gracious and specific to our customer, guest, or fellow employee, but using the name always beats that alternative of "Hey you," "Excuse me," or "Flyers fan" (Philly fan in a jersey). Of course, "Excuse me, sir" or "Pardon me, miss" are great options if you don't have access to or know your guest's name. If a guest gives you their name, please try to use it. This is a "gimme" that gets dropped all the time.

I know, from my own experience, I have tended to *not* use a guest's name when I:

- **Was *almost* sure of it**

- **Forgot it completely**

- **Was unsure of the pronunciation**

We have all been in this position. You don't even have to have worked in hospitality to understand. This is life. I spent years avoiding some people's names because of these three situations. It was simply fear. I didn't want to put myself in that awkward position or embarrass myself. What's worse is the person who always calls you by your name and you awkwardly just say hi back because you can't remember their name. You are not alone!

I always forget: *Oh, I can simply ask them their name again!* There is no rulebook. Even if I may have forgotten it, it's OK. Give yourself a break. You are allowed to ask someone their name again! Everyone can relate to this situation. Now, I just make sure I write it down in my phone notes or on paper after the second time they tell me, so I can reference it.

USING THE OTHER PERSON'S NAME NATURALLY IS ONE OF THE MOST IMPORTANT ELEMENTS OF INTERACTION IN HOSPITALITY.

My buddy Jeremy still doesn't use his neighbor's name because he can't remember it and feels bad—for ten years! (Who can't relate to this one?!) And the same guy calls Jeremy, Jimmy. Jeremy went on too long allowing the misuse of his name—and feels it's too late to correct the guy. (Who can't relate to this as well?)

We all get a little odd around the use, misuse, or non-use of names. Remember, it's OK to ask!

Remembering names is easier when you have the name on the screen in front of you. In fast food and fast casual, we may have the ability to put the guest's name in the computer, and it will populate on the screen, where our team member will call out either the guest's name or number. I'm always amazed at restaurants that use reservation systems such as Resy, OpenTable, or other software that has a guest's name in the computer, right there in front of the host, and they choose not to use it. These are all tools that allow us to connect with the guest. People like to hear their name and enjoy being recognized as an individual—if you use it naturally.

You can always ask, "What is your name, again?" or "How would you like me to address you?" or "Your name was..." Just make a good effort to write it down and remember it so you don't have to ask the same person for their name multiple times. Using the guest's name will make them connected to you, and that is what we are looking for: to make a connection when we provide our service to them.

7

Keep 'Em Coming Back

Making A Connection and Having Guests Return

Delivering consistent, attention-driven service keeps people coming back, and that is a major goal for any business owner. To keep customers, an employer may put into place several methods and programs, which I want to share with you. In my experience, the best way to achieve customer loyalty is by forming a genuine connection with your guests.

The Great Connection

You must try to connect, to help others. I can teach you this, but it helps if you have a desire somewhere in you that gets pleasure from helping others. This is what we do. We are reaching out to others, being proactive, and trying to make a great experience for our guests. Even if that experience is a one or two-minute interaction. This is what sets us apart from other industries.

Doug Washington, a seasoned hospitality veteran from the Bay Area, told me this story. He was doing interviews for a restaurant, and he wanted to put two elderly people on the sidewalk, looking at a map just outside the door of the restaurant. They would pretend to be looking at the map and staring around, clearly giving the impression they were lost.

Now, any server who was coming in for an interview would have to pass these two people to get to the door. If they didn't stop to ask if they could help them, then that could be an indicator that this person was not innately inclined to read the situation, help strangers, and go out of their way to put others first. When he told me this idea, he had never put it into action, but I thought it was an interesting test.

CHANGE LIVES THROUGH ENGAGING WITH PEOPLE. EYE CONTACT, A WARM SMILE, AND A THOUGHTFUL COMMENT.

People have said that you can't teach that instinct to help others. I completely disagree. I feel that it may take time and require a lot of effort, but that we are all capable of using our innate skill of caring for another person, fine-tuning it, and building that small instinct into a bigger skill or craft we can use to help others. Big words, I know. I've seen so many people blossom into amazing service professionals. Sure, they were a little rough at first—as was I—but if you have a drive to hone the craft of connecting with people, then hospitality is a great industry.

We are always coming back to the service point of connecting with guests and co-workers and trying to change lives through engaging with people. Eye contact, a warm smile, and a thoughtful comment. The desire to make something an interaction as opposed to an unenthusiastic transaction. These are some of the ways we reach out to people to let them know they are taken care of.

Maybe this is the only moment in a guest's day where they don't have to take care of someone, answer a question, send an email, or juggle their child's schedule. A brief moment where they can get away from their computer and home office and say hi to another human being. We have this ability to make a quick but solid impact on our guests' lives...day to day. That's an awesome gift to be able to give to someone. If you can keep reminding yourself to connect with each guest for just a couple of seconds, that connection won't just improve their day, but probably yours as well.

Returning Guests

One of my old bosses used to say, "Keep 'em coming back!" That's how it works. Restaurant owners want two things: they want their guests to return and to continue to buy products from this company and not the competition down the street. From this viewpoint, they come up with tactics to bring guests back: keep the prices competitive, ensure customers feel valued, give great service, and maintain quality products. Three of these apply directly to us, the front-facing counter servers.

RESTAURANT OWNERS WANT TWO THINGS: THEY WANT THEIR GUESTS TO RETURN AND TO CONTINUE TO BUY PRODUCTS FROM THIS COMPANY AND NOT THE COMPETITION DOWN THE STREET.

Before loyalty programs existed, the simple rules of thumb were: be nice; be inviting; accommodate your customers' needs; and have fair prices. I'm amazed at the businesses that have forgotten these tenets and replaced them with a punch card for a free drink. As if the hope of a free mocha alone is going to keep the guest returning daily. It's not. Don't be fooled. You must offer great service consistently, and if you combine a loyalty option, great.

Some businesses will build loyalty by offering guests discounts or by getting them on an email list to notify them of deals. This is why some bosses may require you to ask for each guest's phone number, email, or rewards number. They may want to ask guests to join a loyalty program. The purpose of programs like this is so your guests can be notified of new products, sales, specials, and seasonal offerings. The ultimate goal is to make them feel valued and keep 'em coming back.

Owners and marketing teams put a lot of work into targeted ads or publicity. By the time you are presented with a new food or beverage product, months of work may have gone into its development and marketing. It's the job of the counter server to push that new product towards our guests, so they know we are always trying to bring new, quality-driven products to them. Your company wants to offer new experiences to its guests. It's a group effort to have a successful company, and it's important to see how your role fits into the whole picture.

BE NICE; BE INVITING; ACCOMMODATE YOUR CUSTOMERS' NEEDS; AND HAVE FAIR PRICES.

Competition is always trying to take your customers away. In bigger cities, there is competition on every corner. Coffee spots are all over. They will open on the same block, in the same neighborhood. Fast food and fast-casual restaurants open all the time—in short walks or quick drives from one another. Think of all the other types of businesses with nearby competition: grocery stores, banks, gas stations, bars, pharmacies, electronics stores...why would someone *choose* to come back to us? When the owners and managers tell you, "Keep 'em coming back," they are very aware of how easy it is for a customer to take a left turn one day, see a new spot, and never walk back through your business's doors.

Consistency of service is huge factor as well. We have long days in restaurants. It's easy to be great in the first half of the day and then let our standards slide as the day and shift wear on. We can't do that in hospitality. We need to bring our energy consistently during that eight-hour shift. A guest who comes in at four p.m. should receive the same upbeat energy and attention as they would if they came in at eight a.m. It's a challenge in all restaurants. The midafternoon slump, the tired staff at the end of the night, the "fumble in the fourth." If you can maintain your service standards consistently throughout your shift, you are on the road to make sure your guests come back.

Recently, my friend Joe, who works at a wonderful winery, told me that he likes to thank people from the get-go. As they sit down for a tasting: "Thank you for coming in." "Thank you for joining us, we appreciate it." He says it's important to let them know he truly appreciates them and the fact that they chose his winery rather than the forty others they could have chosen. I couldn't agree more. Appreciating your guests is one of the best ways to build a connection with them, and in that process, your great service is building a loyal guest forever. Say thank you and mean it. Just make sure you follow it with a goodbye, and you will keep 'em coming back.

8

Learning from Mistakes

The Importance of Double Checking and Always Debriefing

Double-Check

One aspect of service that has consistently derailed my ability to connect and get guests what they want is making mistakes with orders. I've mentioned in a few places the problem with putting the wrong order in, and I want to address a few issues around this. Putting in the wrong order can start a domino effect that can affect each of the positions on your team and the guest experience. By maintaining an awareness of this key issue, you can avoid a lot of hassle.

Putting the order in wrong can happen for a number of reasons. These are some points that can ensure it only happens rarely:

- **Know the menu items well**

- **Check to see if the kitchen is out of certain items and communicate to a manager to adjust the menu items in the POS system to reflect that**

- Don't agree to make adjustments to the order that the kitchen cannot do

- When you make an adjustment to an order, ensure you are putting it in the POS correctly

- Always ask about the guests' allergies and notate it, if appropriate

- Ensure the DECAF is put in as DECAF

- Double-check and clarify the order with the guest

These are some of the issues that can happen when that order goes into the kitchen wrong:

- The runner has to have an awkward moment at the counter/table as they realize the order is wrong

- The runner, co-worker, or delivery driver has to apologize to person whose order was wrong

- The manager has to determine if they should refund the guest their money (losing the money on the wrong item that was made as well as on the correct item that the manager is now buying for the guest)

- The guest has to wait for their order to be remade correctly while everyone dining with them eats their meals

- The kitchen wastes product and money

- The kitchen has to remake an order

- The other kitchen orders are backed up because they have to remake an order

- **Everyone waits a little longer**

You are then presented with the fallout from the mistaken order if it's not taken care of properly:

- **The guest has a poor dining experience**

- **The waiting guest takes up table space longer than they normally would and other diners can't find a seat, increasing wait times**

- **People around the guest see that the restaurant has messed up an order**

- **The guest is upset and doesn't return to continue buying items from the restaurant**

- **The guest posts a poor review on social media**

Mistakes happen. But as you can see, there are a lot of ways one small mistake can affect all areas of the restaurant. This is why it's important to know your menu, put it in the computer correctly and always DOUBLE-CHECK your orders with the guest before you push Send. And beware: once some guests see a problem, they look for others. The one mistake opens a door for further scrutiny. It's a slippery slope, so pay attention to the details and try to avoid making crucial mistakes.

Debrief

I've always found it useful and essential to ask myself or our teams, how did I do? How did **we** do? What can I do better? Where can I set myself up for success a little better for the next time we get slammed, have a few co-workers call out of work, or have an unhappy guest? This doesn't always have to be in a quick group meeting after work, honestly, time doesn't usually permit this. Most employees leave at staggered "Out times" toward the end of the night. The crucial aspect of the idea of Debriefing is the conversation you have with yourself.

Can I set myself up better for tomorrow? Can I work more efficiently or prepare a little better for when that unexpected moment arrives? It's important that this debrief happens as soon as you end your shift. It's always good to take a quick moment and write down a note or play a situation back in your head. If you wait too long, you will forget about it or naturally your mind will move onto your after-work activities. Take a brief moment and see if there is anything you think you can do differently next time that will make your job a little easier.

WHAT CAN I DO BETTER? WHERE CAN I SET MYSELF UP FOR SUCCESS A LITTLE BETTER FOR THE NEXT TIME WE GET SLAMMED.

In very successful Full-Service restaurants, the end of night "Huddle Up" is essential. I get it, people are tired, they want to go home. But this is where tremendous growth can happen through small moments of reflection and intention. This doesn't have to be a long process. It could take a minute or two. You could also simply jot down a note for yourself or to remember something to share with your team at a later time. Do it while it's fresh in your mind. What's important is to ask the questions: How can I do better? What can we do better as you reflect on the team's day or night's service? The answer is in the details.

PART 2

9

JAYMIE LAO

FORMER DIRECTOR OF CAFÉ EXPERIENCE - GO GET EM TIGER

Jaymie has had a massive influence in the coffee industry through her work as a trainer, leadership coach and coffee professional. She's served as a leader at iconic coffee places in Los Angeles like Go Get Em Tiger, G&B Coffee, and Intelligentsia.

Service

You have to have an interest in what is happening behind the bar, looking into the details of what happens, even if you don't know how to make coffee. [You need] a genuine interest in service, not just the product, because at this point what sets a lot of coffee shops apart *is* the service. Not to say that the coffee or the product doesn't matter as much, but I think everyone in the industry buys coffee from a lot of the same producers. So, the way you stand out is: you potentially roast it differently or better than another coffee company, or you have exceptional service!

Read the Room

The part of the job that's really difficult is the human component. It is talking to people, getting people excited about the product, or just talking to people about their day. Once you become an expert at tasting, preparing coffee, and understanding what is happening from beginning to end, then you get to focus on just the service, on just connecting with whoever's around you. A customer or another coworker—to be able to hear someone that you're working with who might need help or support. Working on a team is like a sport, right? You have to be reading the room and understanding what anyone on the floor—customer or fellow employee—is doing at any given point in time.

Feedback

Displaying openness to receiving feedback carries a lot more weight than what's on the résumé. When you listen to someone talk about their past experiences, you can kind of get a sense of... if they were to leave this company, how would they speak about us to their future employers, and is that the kind of person that would do well in this space? It's so important that you, as an employee, can both receive feedback well and dole it out well. And that is something that your people have to be trained to do. It's not that anyone has to be perfect at it, but displaying openness to growing by way of feedback is important.

Baristatude

It is really difficult to find a balanced barista. Someone who loves the details of coffee as much as they love the service aspect. People can be so engrossed in the coffee process they forget about the customer experience. You can tell when someone is only interested in the latte art—in that presentation—and not about how it makes other people feel. They're only interested in how it makes themselves feel: accomplished. You can feel accomplished in different ways when you're in service, but that latte art can't be the only thing that makes you feel that way. You have to be excited about hospitality. It can't just be coffee and coffee art, because then you run the risk of becoming the stereotype of a barista—someone who is going to judge, kind of make you feel like bad when you walk away. That is a stereotype, yeah, and there's like, you know, handlebar mustaches attached to it, and newsboy caps—the whole nine yards.

But if you crush on service, you can dress however you want. If you already know how to make coffee, then you're delivering all the goods. I feel like the industry as a whole has grown towards being more service-focused and not, like, "Look at me, let me tell you the entire story of this farm," which is also important, but is maybe not what the customer is expecting. Unless they ask for it, right?

Seeing the Whole Space

At Go Get 'Em Tiger, staff are trained to consider the whole store, not just what's inside the store—any way that a customer can experience the store. If they're walking up to it, is there trash on the sidewalk? Is the music loud enough to not be annoying, but to draw someone closer to the space? Wherever it is that someone can be interacted with, you have to take that into consideration and know service can extend up to that point. It's not, "Oh, service begins when you enter the doorway." Service actually begins when you're in my line of vision.

And if I'm standing on the patio at the Los Feliz location, and I see you running across the street or I see you dropping your kid off at the Conservatory of Music, I could be striking up a conversation that allows me to know what you want before you even enter this space. Or maybe you're someone who always comes in after you drop off your kid, and I can holler to my coworkers, "Hey, start that cappuccino right now." And by the time you get in, it's ready. It's there for you. And that's the kind of service that I love giving, and it's such an easy win for everybody. When staff see the reaction from that, it should motivate them to continue to give that sort of service and figure out how to give that service to everyone.

Read the Play

Not everyone is going to want that [kind of service], because some people don't want to be cornered into always having a cappuccino every day. You want to have the ability to pivot to a different drink because maybe it's really hot outside and they want an iced tea. It's about being able to read the room, read the play.

The Spirit of Saying Yes

You have to find how you can say yes. In coffee it can be challenging. If someone were to order a hemp milk latte and your cafe doesn't have hemp milk, obviously, you cannot say yes, but you now know what the customer's expectation or need is. If someone is ordering that, clearly they're avoiding dairy. So don't recommend dairy. Let them know what you *can* do for them. It's not because you don't want to give them the thing they want, but you literally cannot produce it for them. Try to find a way of saying yes, offering alternatives. Working in the spirit of saying yes is really important to the overall principles of service.

Saying yes is one of the most powerful and also scary principles of service, because when open to interpretation, people think that this is meant to not allow employees to have boundaries, but there are actually very clear boundaries. When you say yes, you are communicating what the limitation is and what you can do for them within that framework.

Authenticity

Service comes from you. In a lot of counter-sales service, things can sound very robotic, it can sound very scripted. The best service that happens is the one that feels most natural to you. It's a really important principle of service.

Steps vs. Principles

The principles of service aren't necessarily like the steps of service. There [are] the steps of service, where you want to make sure that you are hitting all the different milestones of a transaction, and then there's the principles of service that allow you to understand how you can deliver the steps and troubleshoot.

High Level of Service

Everyone deserves the same level of service, but everyone wants it differently. A high-level service can be different for each person: there could be someone who wants to have that really long conversation with you about, you know, the last episode of *Game of Thrones,* and then there's the person who walks in and just wants their coffee and [wants] to leave. And when you meet those people exactly where they want you to—*that is the same level of service.* Not everyone requires, like, a three-minute conversation, and not everyone just wants a to-go drink immediately, but to recognize that is definitely a skill and something that people work towards.

Dinner-Party Vibes

So much of the service style [At Go Get Em Tiger] was meant to be bar-style. You are acknowledging the order in which people come in, but when you're having a conversation with one person, you have to be having it with everyone. There are no secret conversations. If I'm serving you and then someone walks in, I'm going to talk loudly enough that this person is part of it, and I'm going to look at them and make sure they know that I'm also describing this drink to not just you, but to that person as well. And that helps to make someone feel included, when maybe they just happened to walk into a conversation. So definitely like dinner-party vibes, like letting people interject at any point, while still giving a high level of service.

How You Treat Each Other and Yourself

This is not just about the service that you give to guests, it is also the service that you give to your co-workers and trying to make sure that the way that people interact with each other behind the bar [is] not dissimilar from the way that they would interact with people on the other side. People can complain about whatever they want, but I think that it's a waste of breath when you're at work - to do that and to upset yourself.

Acknowledging People When They Walk In

[I want] immediate acknowledgment, knowing that you see me when I walk into the space, or to know you are ready to receive me when I'm ready, because maybe I don't know what I want to order. Sometimes you can walk into a café or anywhere, and you can see that the staff are more interested in talking to each other then they are talking to whoever is walking in. As much as I really love workspaces where people truly enjoy each other, if you can't drop that conversation for another time and acknowledge someone walking in, that is really detrimental to service. I don't need to be greeted "Good morning" immediately, and I don't have to have my order taken immediately. But if I'm walking into the space and I see a little head nod or just eye contact, that makes me immediately less anxious about being in the space and wondering, "Do they see me? Am I allowed in here? Am I interrupting something?" I'm not necessarily looking out for that when I go into cafés, but when I don't receive that acknowledgment, as a human, I think, "Do they even want me to be here?"

10

READING PEOPLE

PAYING ATTENTION TO NON-VERBAL COMMUNICATION

My wife, Kirsten, has never been a big fan of me saying, "I know what you're thinking." And then I follow it with what I think she is thinking. For the record, I do not have a degree in mind reading, I'm not a psychic, and to the best of my knowledge, I do not possess any supernatural abilities. When I do express what I think she is thinking, it can be often met with a raised eyebrow, a quick shake of the head, or arms crossed. Because I'm clearly wrong. Hopefully I don't get all three signs at once, because that would be bad news. To which, I quickly rephrase the question and ask, "What do you think?" "Any thoughts?" or "How are you feeling?"

What I *can* pick up from that interaction is Kirsten raising her eyebrow, crossing her arms, or shaking her head. That is called "nonverbal communication." She doesn't say anything; she doesn't have to. I can draw some conclusions from her movements. Nonverbal signs are indications that may tell us how someone is feeling without saying anything. And all of us should practice the skills to read them. We all have the skills; we just need to hone them and pay attention with how they can help us be of service.

We've been doing it since we were babies. Before we could even understand spoken language, we picked up on these signs. Certainly because of safety and survival. But also, to get what we need. If you have a phone, look up emojis or GIFs; those can be great examples of nonverbal communication. Have you looked at one to try to figure out what it means? Happy, sad, mad, frustrated, excited. The list goes on, as do the endless GIFs we text each other to tell each other how we feel. And we are surrounded by them every day.

NONVERBAL SIGNS ARE INDICATIONS THAT MAY TELL US HOW SOMEONE IS FEELING WITHOUT SAYING ANYTHING. AND ALL OF US SHOULD PRACTICE THE SKILLS TO READ THEM.

We see nonverbal cues from people all the time. Some examples of positive nonverbal communication (my wife does these ones too!) are people smiling, running to each other with open arms, hugging, putting a hand on a shoulder, shaking hands, nodding while making eye contact and smiling. On the flip side, we can see when people are in need: distressed, annoyed, and frustrated. A few examples may be a stressed person pacing and gesturing wildly with their hands, an annoyed person with their arms crossed in the doctor's office waiting room, or a little kid, shoulders slumped and crying because he just found out he's not tall enough to ride Space Mountain at Disneyland.

We pick these cues up from our family, closest friends, girlfriends, boyfriends, and partners all the time. Being aware of these types of communication—and most importantly, actively looking for these signs—is essential in food and beverage service. If we can start to actively read the nonverbal signs of our guests and customers, we can start to anticipate their needs before they have to ask us. We can address an issue before they have to bring it to our attention. This is what can set you far apart from others in customer service. It's a skill that is learned and honed throughout your life.

Our goal in restaurants is to ensure our guests have a good experience with us. So, if we have guests showing signs of distress and we aren't paying attention to those nonverbal cues, we run the risk of losing those guests' return business. Some common examples that may be a sign you should check in with a guest include:

- **Squinting and straining to read a menu on the board**

- **Rolling their eyes**

- **Crossing arms**

- **Making a frustrated face**

- **Shaking their head**

- **Pursing lips**

- **Breath shortening**

It can be harder to read people who are seated at a table. In addition to the list above, some good indications you should go check on seated guests are:

- **Not touching their food**

- **Looking around for someone/something**

- **Arms crossed at the table with a concerned look on their face**

Great servers are very aware of their guests' nonverbal cues. If you want to exceed your guests' expectations, the anticipation of their needs will do it every time. Ideally, if you can get something for a guest before they have to ask you for it, you will win that interaction every time. It's an amazing skill. And most people are very thankful for that type of caring and attention-based service.

Here are a few exercises you can use to hone this skill:

- **Watch TV with the sound off and see if you can guess what** they are talking about. Body language can tell you a whole story. Rewind and see if you are correct.

- GIF scroll. Type an emotion into your GIF search engine and see what comes up. These are excessive but are usually pretty good indicators of feelings.

Put your headphones on and sit in a park, on a bus, or a public place where people are talking and see what you can tell by their physical expressions.

11

ERIK OBERHOLTZER

---◈◈◈---

FOUNDER - TENDER GREENS

Many years ago, the first fast casual/quick service restaurant experience I was completely amazed by was Tender Greens. I was stunned by the knowledge of the counter servers and the "dining experience" they offered in such a quick amount of time. Eric Oberholtzer is the Co-founder of this nationally recognized fast casual industry leader.

Accommodating Guests

I think that the sense of pride and enthusiasm is the spirit and passion for taking care of everyone who comes in, without ego or restrictions. There was a time when a chef wouldn't cook a steak well done or put a burger on the menu because that interfered with his ego. Coming out of luxury, there was a standard of "Yes is the answer; what is the question?" Meaning, we can always accommodate any request, within reason. We may not be able to accommodate the exact request, but we are going to get as close as we can.

There is a sense of pride and talent in the chefs in all our restaurants. If we have the ingredients, we certainly have the skills to accommodate, and we will do it. We are not robotic, and we are here to give the guest a great experience. Though we are focused on a curated menu and believe that our combinations are the best variation, we are still going to do whatever we can to make sure you have the experience you want.

Turn it into a Win

I started my career with the Four Seasons, and a part of the culture there—part of the challenge—is "give us the most difficult guest and we will turn them into our most committed and long-term customer." If we can accommodate someone who might seem high-maintenance—if we can smile, have fun with it, get to know them. [Then we can] turn something that otherwise might be negative into a challenge, and then win that person over in the challenge and have fun with it.

Getting through a Lunch Rush

It starts with [finding] the right person that has the stamina to get through a busy lunch. Not everyone can do it. Not everyone wants or is willing to do it. You need the right person to get through that intense, grueling lunch rush—day in and day out. And sometimes under crazy conditions. It's hot; sometimes the POS system goes down; sometimes there is food that comes back, or a complaint. Many things are thrown at you.

Announcing Food Tableside

At the minimum, it's "This is the salad Niçoise with the vegetable and mashed potato." You are repeating the order back. Much like at the cashier, where you may repeat the order, you want to make sure this is the correct dish the person is looking at. So, they *hear it* and *see it* at the *same time*. If the guest has questions and they want information of what is on the plate, we can go deep into that description as well: "It's an endive from X farms, it's organic, and it came in this morning."

Checking Back

The follow-up after dropping the food at the table should be checking in with the guest on how they're doing, a little bit of upselling, or both. We will offer another beer if they are at the end of theirs or ask them if they would like a refill on their lemonade. We try to give as much tableside hospitality without turning it into a full tableside experience, because it's not necessary to the expectation of the guest or the staffing level.

Honoring the Quality of Food

Our food and product philosophy is probably a little bit more severe than most brands. We know where ingredients come from, why it matters, and the inherent value on the plate because of the quality and the cost of the ingredients. We honor that, and the more sophisticated guest that is interested in the fact that a food item was grown twenty-five minutes from the restaurant, on the patio, or that it's grass-fed rather than grain fed.

Managing the Point-of-Sale (POS) System

We don't throw someone on the POS system right away. They will bus tables, do drinks, work in a support role first so they can learn things and the flow of the restaurant, supported by training, structure, and classes.

Our Deal

The baseline of the deal between you and me is: I'm going to pay you a wage, give you a free meal, a uniform, and you are going to come in and do a job. And the expectations of the job are very clear. And you either do that job to standard or you don't. Or you go above and beyond that standard and put yourself in a position to advance. That's the transactional part. Our responsibility is to pay you, take care of you, set you up for success.

Advancement

The brand view is: we are going believe in you in the spirit of partnership. So, if you do want to advance, we are going to help you along. If you find you have a passion for food, or a passion for pasta salad, or a passion for business, and you want to learn more, you might even contemplate doing this for a career. Then we can partner with you on that. We can build a career with you. And you have an opportunity to be a part of something bigger than yourself.

"Be a Random Act of Kindness" Sign on the Way Out the Door

It's meant for everybody. The idea for that is a parting thought as you leave the restaurant. So, if you are walking down the street or to your car, or whatever you are doing in your day—that you might show up with some kindness, whether it's to someone you walk by on the street or letting someone take their turn in the car and not cutting them off. It's a little intentionality without being preachy. It's open-ended.

12

FEEDBACK

---⊂⧫⊃---

GIVING AND RECEIVING CONSTRUCTIVE FEEDBACK WITH EMPLOYEES, MANAGERS, AND GUESTS

There are so many different ways you might receive feedback and direction. Feedback. Constructive feedback. Getting told what to do better. Getting told what to do again. Getting told how to do something the right way. Getting told how to do something in a new way. Getting told a second time to do something. Getting told that you're not doing something correctly. Getting yelled at (not very constructive!) for not doing something correctly. Good grief!

It is important for us to be open to hearing any feedback given to us without immediately becoming defensive, angry, sad, overwhelmed, annoyed, frustrated, or revengeful. Filter out what can get in your way of taking the constructive note. We all have that voice in our head that can show up and start telling us a different narrative than what is actually happening in the moment. For example, *I can't believe he said that to me in front of everyone. I can't believe she had the audacity to tell me that. I work so hard here, this is disrespectful, and I am shocked that person would give me a note like that.* We come up with all these stories that are signs of feeling defensive and not wanting to take the constructive note. We aren't giving ourselves the space to hear the feedback.

I've had some hard bosses, but once I was able to focus on just the note aspect of the feedback, not the HOW it was delivered, I found myself in a much better place to adjust my behavior and grow.

Constructive feedback is not always delivered the way we would like it. You may feel all those feelings I just told you to put on hold. I'm not saying not to feel those. That's human behavior and completely understandable. But when we jump into those feelings and hold on tight to those initial reactions, that can cloud our ability to understand the information that is being given. In a way, we have to learn how to constructively listen. A good friend told me that in times like these where he is feeling defensive, he will actively change his thought from "I can't believe this is happening TO me" to "I can't believe this is happening FOR me." Changing how he looks at the information being given. That it is a gift and a chance to adjust and move forward with direction, while turning his negative viewpoint into a positive one.

Feedback is essential to innovation, and even the people delivering it struggle with the best way to give it. It can be difficult to figure out the best way to make sure a point is thoroughly understood and comprehended. The reason we use the word *constructive* is that we always want to make sure that we are giving feedback in a way that helps someone do the work better, understand, and retain the details of the tasks that are being addressed. A great teacher is able to ensure the information lands with all types of different learners. If we are in a position to coach or give direction, some thoughtfulness needs to go into planning this encounter.

Of course, there will be training and shadowing that happens during service while guests are present, but when you have to have a serious conversation it's important to take a few things into account:

- **Finding the right time to give constructive feedback:** The right time might not be when the restaurant is overwhelmed and has a line out the door, the end of a stressful eight-hour shift, or while an employee is already feeling defensive about their performance. You might find it benefits you to wait until the end of the shift or even the next day.

- **Finding the right place and situation:** As an employee, I've had notes or been scolded in front of other co-workers, and my embarrassment led me to be more defensive toward my manager. Picking the right place to have the private meeting or interaction will benefit your feedback process.

- **Being in a good emotional space to give constructive notes and feedback:** If you are coming from a purely emotional place, a heated situation, or a tense shift of service, you may forget to focus on the actions and their effects as opposed to possibly attacking employee's personality. You want to set yourself up for a successful interaction the best you can.

A company is always trying to improve their services, and this feedback is part of the process. The goal of any company is to continue to be profitable and make money: money for its owners, shareholders, and employees. To make money, a company must innovate, adjust, and keep its employees informed. This all takes a process of learning and cannot happen without a feedback circle existing between co-workers, management, and ownership.

I still have to remind myself that that feedback is a part of the process and not an attack on me. I oftentimes have to quiet that critical voice in my head. I will get constructive feedback on this book, and I will probably feel a little defensive. But it's an essential part of the process of improving. This is how craftspeople teach the craft. When you're learning the craft, you are going to fail in the process, learn some more, then do it better the next time. Those are the moments you build on. And soon you are performing at a higher level, consistently.

The ability to give and receive feedback and to show that you understand the benefits of this concept will help you in this job and in your future jobs. I say *give* as well as *receive* because they are both difficult to do well. These will both be a part of your process as you grow in this business and take on more responsibilities.

Guest Feedback

On occasion you may be on the other side of some constructive feedback that doesn't feel very constructive. A guest annoyed and raising their voice at you because the fries weren't made as crispy as they wanted them is going to fall into the "Deconstructive feedback" pile for me. A guest yelling at you because their latte doesn't have enough milk in it will fall into that pile as well. A guest asking you, "Are you stupid?" in regard to you not knowing that the Iced Tea would run out is not constructive feedback.

I have little tolerance for this type of behavior from a guest. If you notice, there are key words in the phrases above. "Raising their voice," "Yelling," "Stupid." These aren't behaviors that are used to give constructive criticism. And often times this type of behavior may quickly grow to an unacceptable level, where you may need to leave the situation and/or get a manager immediately. Have I been on the other side of these? Yes, for sure. I've had unhappy guests say and do all of these to me. You have a choice to make in this situation. How do you want to respond? Here are a few tips on how to respond in a situation where the guest is becoming increasingly agitated, verbally abusive and going beyond constructive feedback. These are in no particular order.

- **Do not escalate the situation**: Stay calm in the situation, let them finish what they are saying, and don't try to meet them with the same behavior they may be using.

- **Allow the guest to give you the solution to their issue**: "While I understand you are unhappy, please let me know how you would like me to fix the situation."

- **Reassure the guest you have heard them and are taking care of the**

situation: Take a breath, repeat back what the guest has just said, "So you are saying you would like me to have them remake your fries and ensure they are extra crispy? Let me see what I can do for you."

- **If their behavior is upsetting and you need to leave immediately let the guest know you are getting someone to help**: "I'm so sorry we made you feel that way. You are clearly upset. Please give me a moment to get a manager to assist us with this situation."

- **Address the behavior, while setting boundaries with the guest**: "I would like to provide you with good service, but I'm not able to do so while you are treating me disrespectfully."

- **If you need to exit immediately**: "Please excuse me for a moment." Leave the situation and find a supervisor or manager to assist you with the guest.

13

Jo Galvan

Ray Kroc award winner - McDonald's Manager

Jo Galvan is a recipient of the national Ray Croc award, one of the highest awards given to top managers in the McDonald's Fast-Food company. She worked for McDonalds for 23 years and was most recently the manager of a McDonald's store in Monaco, Pennsylvania.

Life Skills

Some of these kids really have never been out of their bedrooms on a weekend. They're playing with their Xbox or Facetiming—they're in their own little world. This [type of] work just breaks them out of that shell—their eyes are just opened. We're teaching them to make eye contact, ask questions, seek out answers. We are teaching responsibility: *This is how you check your schedule. I expect you to be here five minutes early.* How to put your stuff away, get ready, punch in, ask your manager where you are going.

We have kids that started here when they [were] fourteen that are now seventeen. There is one, my goodness, she's wonderful. Once she graduates this year, she's going to be seventeen years old, and she's going to be an assistant manager. I remember her first day and she said, "I don't know what to do." And I said, "It's OK, come here, I'll show you." Just seeing how far she came. She will tell you, "I just didn't know anything, my mom didn't care what time I went to bed, she didn't care what time I woke up, she didn't care about A, B, C, or D. I just learned that I need to be responsible for myself and take some accountability for my actions, you know." The impact is indescribable, it really is. And I know for a fact when she is walking for her graduation, I will be there with bells on, probably with my family. I am so proud of her. And I want her to know, I've always been her support and I always have her back.

Connections in Other Cities

I have an employee here right now. She goes to school here, so she works for me when she's in school. She also takes advantage of McDonald's tuition assistance ($2,500), which is awesome. And then when she goes home—she lives about an hour and a half from here—she works at the McDonald's up there when she's up there. And she's a shift runner up there too. I'm really proud of her.

Hiring

I would say ninety percent of our applications come online. We have an automated system called McHire, and there's a bot that talks to you, Olivia. She gets basic information: name, birthdate, where you went to school, if you graduated, if you're currently a student, stuff like that. When she kicks out their interview information, she also sets that up for them. She picks the time. We have a full calendar set up.

Dress

First impressions are very important, and you always want to make a good one. Some people come in with their ripped jeans and boots, their hair all crazy and six-inch fingernails on—that's not professional. Maybe if you're going to work or apply at a bar or something, that may be appropriate. I don't judge anybody. I will interview anybody that comes in because everybody deserves a chance. We definitely give everybody a shot. If you look put together, or at least make an effort, that's what I'm looking for. If you come in here and you can talk to me and make eye contact with me, then we can have those conversations. Like, "I love your nails, but they may not be quite appropriate for food handling." And then, if they're interested in the job, they have a good interview, and I want to hire them, then we go over the expectations for everything.

LISTEN, WE CAN'T ALWAYS BE FAST. OUR FOCUS IS CUSTOMER SERVICE AND THE CUSTOMER EXPERIENCE AND HOSPITALITY. THAT'S WHAT'S GOING TO KEEP PEOPLE COMING BACK.

Positions

We have a lot of crew positions. Front Counter involves the ringing of the order, sometimes getting the order together, calling out the order numbers and delivering them, and seeing that the customer has everything, making sure they are OK.

We have the Order Taking and then some secondary duties like the person who gets the orders together for Drive-Thru, and even French fries are considered a service. Then we have the Back Cash Booth, which is the first actual physical impression that you get of the business because the customers are at the speakers, order, and then they pull around [to the Back Cash Booth]. It's fast-paced; we have to move this line, and you want to be nice and fast. Make sure you can fix anything that may be wrong. And then we have the Front Window, which is to present the food, hand out the order, greet them with a smile.

There are some McDonald's that have the speaker and also have someone outside doing the handheld order taking on a tablet. If you have a card, you can pay right there, you don't have to stop at the [Back Cash Booth] window. The only time you would have to stop is to pick up your food unless you are paying with cash.

Initial Onboarding

On the very first day, we sit with [new hires] and go over food safety—probably about an hour. Next is the OSHA information—about an hour. Then hospitality, and we finish with the safe workplace and harassment information. These are the four things that McDonald's does not slack on. We have a training piece on hospitality that we have them watch their very first day before they do anything else. It shows proper greetings and different things. How to speak to your manager or how to speak to your peers, and how to speak to customers.

Greetings

It's "Hi, how are you, may I take your order?" Or "Hi, may I take your order?" Anything with a smile, short and to the point. As you see them coming in, if they're pushing a baby stroller, "Oh hey, let me get that door for you!" and offer to open the door. If somebody has a big, heavy order, "Can I help carry that to the table for you?" We don't stress the *ma'am* and *sir*. It's just a simple "Yes, I can help you" or "No, I can't, let me find somebody who can." It's about how to approach people: always with a smile, simple and to the point, and help when you can.

Being Nice

On the weekends, it's sometimes a little bit hard to move the drive and inside orders because there are big orders. High volume. Sometimes we have families of six, seven, or eight sitting in the dining room ordering $50, $60, $70 meals, so things can tend to back up a little bit. The one thing I tell everybody is, "Listen, we can't always be fast. Our focus is customer service and the customer experience and hospitality. That's what's going to keep people coming back." Are sales important? Absolutely. I have to pay my people, have to maintain the building; we have bills to pay and stuff like that. But if our service isn't 100 percent and we are mean to somebody or we come off rude or annoyed—then they're not going to come back next week. But, if we're a little bit slower, and we take a minute, make sure that we're getting it right, we're smiling and we're saying, "Thank you, please come back." We are checking on them at the table: "Hi, is there anything I can take?" "Do you need a refill?" Things like that. Just little tiny things. The guest may say, "Maybe they weren't the quickest today but, my God, they were so nice. I think we are going to go back there next weekend." The best advice I can give: just stay positive, take a breath, and just [do] one thing at a time.

Supervisory Roles

I had a lot of bad experiences with managers, and I don't ever want anybody to feel like I made them feel like they weren't good enough, weren't smart enough, or didn't matter to me. We do have a few under-eighteen shift managers. They must go through a management interview. We ask them about different scenarios. *Can you relate to this situation? What if you have to correct your friend?* You may not be as authoritative as you need to be, because that's your friend, as opposed to how you would handle somebody that you are cordial with. Are you going to handle that the same way or differently? Because if it's not the same way, then you are not ready to be a manager.

You absolutely cannot have favoritism. You have to treat everybody fairly. And if that pulls you out of your comfort zone, then good—you are learning something. It's not always going to be sunshine and rainbows. Sometimes you have to have the tough conversation. So, if you are not OK stepping out of that comfort zone, taking a chance, if you're not ready for that, then you are not ready to be on the management team. Things might go bad, and they might go well—but you're never going to know until we have that conversation. It's a learning experience here every day.

14

MAKE IT MEAN SOMETHING

FINDING MEANING AND MOTIVATION IN YOUR JOB

Kirsten has often suggested, let's get something on the books, so we have something to look forward to. So, that's what we do. Maybe it's a day trip or a date night, or a one-night, two-day vacation an hour away from our home, or a sporting event. We like to have something to look forward to because it helps us if we are having a tough week at work...we have a great thing to focus on.

Day trips are plentiful on the West Coast, so I know a lot of people who will make plans for their day off and head to the beach to swim or chill, the mountains to hike, and the desert to relax. It sure helps when you are giving so much in your job, and you need a little me-time to relax and recharge. Having something to look forward to helps people get through some of those tougher days at work.

Hopefully you are lucky, and the intrinsic duties of the job motivate and excite you. But if they don't—you certainly aren't alone. It's important to ask yourself why you are doing this job. Maybe it's as simple as *I need to buy groceries, pay rent and tuition, or have spending cash*. Most of us do our jobs to pay bills, but if you can start to layer in other reasons, you may find yourself feeling a little more positive about your job.

I've met a lot of young professionals who put themselves into counter-style jobs because they knew it would force them to get better at speaking in front of people. The two-minute interaction isn't a daunting situation, and yet you get used to speaking in front of people and engaging with guests.

Personally, I always enjoyed the job because I liked to meet new people. It was a great way to make friends and interact with people from different walks of life. I've had a lot of diverse jobs in hospitality, and I'm still friends with people from all those businesses. Working with different teams has always improved my social life when I moved to a new area or was at a transitional point in my life.

Learning about people will always help you in your own pursuits. One of the things I love most about hospitality is it has a revolving set of guests involved, different challenges, and an unlimited opportunity to learn more about engaging with people. Reading people nonverbally, getting better at anticipating needs, multitasking skills, conflict resolution, people skills! I know this doesn't have to just be a clock-in, clock-out job...that I can get more from it if I want.

You are not always going to feel the passion to be of service. I won't lie, when you are a front-facing employee talking to guests all day long, it's going to get tiring. You may feel grumpy walking into the fifth straight day of work. You might be overwhelmed with other things in your life and think, *I just don't want to be here today.* The quickest way out of this rut is to make your job about someone else. Remind yourself you are here to be of service to others. *I'm going to make someone feel better than when they walk in my door.* If you are just simply trying to do that one task, you will have a much more engaging time and fewer boring moments at work. I'm always amazed at the chipper coffee server in our neighborhood at 5:30 a.m. And more amazed that the same person is chipper when I come back for my afternoon coffee at 12:30 p.m.

If you absolutely hate your job, your boss is very mean, and you are disconnected from your co-workers—it's going to be a tall order to find great meaning in that situation. It's certainly not going to be a good situation for guests to walk into.

I've seen it many, many times... I've walked into a café or coffee spot, and it seems like none of the workers are happy to be there. You walk into a restaurant or bar, and your server or bartender looks at you like you ruined their day because you sat in their section. That's a person who doesn't like their job.

Take some time and try to reengage with what you can give and what you can receive from this specific job. Try to dial into giving it some sort of meaning other than the paycheck. Yes, we all would probably rather be at the beach or a backyard barbeque than at work, but giving yourself some reasons to get extra pleasure from your job is a great way to have a more fulfilling work experience. Make a list; keep it in your pocket. If you are feeling crispy, a little disconnected, remind yourself of some other reasons that can inspire you at work. Find a video game you really want to buy, a concert you want to attend, a people skill you want to improve on, something that will reengage you in your job and excite you about coming to work. Make it mean something to you.

15

SEAN PRAMUK

FORMER OWNER - FOOD SHED TAKE AWAY

Sean Pramuk is one of the best Front of House leaders I've met, excelling at training his teams to engage with guests at the two sit-down restaurants he has co-owned in Napa, California. He then transitioned his service standards to a fast casual concept, Food Shed Takeaway, which he operated for many years.

Limited Experience

Most of our kids in [the] front of the house are students. A lot of them are just fresh out of junior year of high school. I don't mind hiring people without experience. I would rather have someone fresh and teach them our way or [what we] consider the right way. Most of our staff is under twenty-five.

Being Firm, but Offering Alternatives

Know your menu, know what we can do, and be confident in saying, "This is what we can offer you. We have a ninety-item menu; what is going to appeal to you? What can we do for you that is going to get you fed?" All of our green salads are already prepared. Chopped salad already has the ham in it. So, a sixty-five-year-old man comes in and asks for a chopped salad with no ham, I've got to have a sixteen-year-old girl with a strong backbone say, "No, the salads are already prepared. It has the ham, we have other salads that don't have ham, but we can't make you one that doesn't have ham in it." We teach [our employees] to say, "No, we don't have *that*, but we do have *this*." We offer [our guests] an alternative suggestion.

As Close as Possible

I tell our staff, "You have to look someone in the eyes, figure out what it is they want, and then try to get them as close to that as possible. Even if it isn't what they initially want." It may not be fun, but you've got to learn this now or later—you might as well learn it now, because [here] it's just about pepperoni pizza. If you can succeed in this, in life—this is going to help you whether you are in restaurants, a venture capitalist, or whatever you decide to do.

> **WE TEACH [OUR EMPLOYEES] TO SAY, "NO, WE DON'T HAVE THAT, BUT WE DO HAVE THIS." WE OFFER [OUR GUESTS] AN ALTERNATIVE SUGGESTION.**

Be Ready

I want you to be able to stay busy—whether that is folding brown pizza boxes or it's picking herbs. When the customer walks in the door—you acknowledge them and watch them, so when they do have that moment of "I have a question" or "I figured this out, I'm ready to go," you are ready for them.

Read the Room

I tell my staff, "You know Malcom Gladwell says we make 600 messages with our body and our face without saying anything." And I just went to New Zealand

and Fiji, and guess what—the body language is the same. The body language that [we] use in America when we are confused, hungry, angry, or whatever is the same body language used in other countries. So, it's up to us to see that, read that! My arms are crossed, and my forehead has a furrowed brow. All these things that say, "Hey, this needs attention, this needs action." We have to intervene here! That is the hardest part, reading that body language and reacting to it. The one thing I repeat over and over is "Read the room. Read the room. Read the room."

Listening to People Over the Phone

On the phone you can't read [people], but you can pick up on their tone—are they hungry, is there a crying baby in the background? Do they need delivery? It's like a game. You have to put all the pieces together. Listen to them; let them rattle on for a bit. Listening is a dying art. It's underrated. You have to maintain the radio voice. "That's not something we offer, but I can read you what we have, or you can check it out online, whatever is easiest for you." What's going to be easiest for you to get this order together?

But you can't turn on them. The most important thing I tell our staff to do is to listen. What is this person looking for? Do they want the food hot? Food cold? They may need to be walked through how the restaurant works. You want to get them on your side and make them feel like you are looking out for their best interest without overselling or gouging them. Again, we try to not use the word *no*; we respond, "I'm sorry, that is not available, but we can offer you this." And have patience. We put our top people on our phone. It is the most challenging position. It's that first impression. It might be the guest's only impression. It is the face of the restaurant.

Great Employee

We have an employee that started out at seventeen and knew nothing. Everyone loves working with her. She soaks up information, she tries her hardest, she [is] always pleasant. Never a mean word. The kind of person everyone wants to work with. It's the greatest attribute. She has picked up all these skills over time.

No Phones

As soon as a customer looks up and sees a staff member on their phone behind the counter—that is a huge negative in my book. It says, "I've got something else going on," as opposed to looking people in the eye, talking to them in a calm and reasonable manner—those are the great skills.

Rolling with It

People are going to make mistakes, whether it's our own staff or the customers. Whether it's all the phones ringing at once or many other things. You will get frazzled. Frustrations are going to occur... it's how you decide to roll with it.

16

KIM PRINCE

--◦❖◦--

FOUNDER/OWNER - HOTVILLE CHICKEN

Yes, Kim is from the family dynasty of Hot Chicken Sandwiches, originating in Nashville, TN. She has had her own amazing restaurant in Los Angeles called Hotville, which has recently teamed with the delicious Dulan's Soul Food restaurant for a food truck, called Dulanville. Kim exemplifies helping people grow and learn in this business.

Follow the Best

I always find it important to say, "Hey, find somebody who is doing what you admire or what you want to be able to do. Surround yourself with people that are like-minded and pick a person that inspires you to follow. And if they're doing it successfully enough or enough to catch your attention, then watch how they maneuver, how they behave, how to answer the phone, how to treat customers, how they do their tasks."

Look to the people who inspire you or that you're admiring, people who are going to influence how you make decisions-how you talk, how you behave at work... and mimic what they do. Stay a little longer so you can ask questions, write down questions that you might have within your head and learn how to grow, how to verbalize or communicate what that question might be and then ask them why they do it. Try to find the little steppingstones that they went through to get to that other side. That's what's going allow you to achieve that type of success or accomplishment or even gain the skill sets that it takes to move up the ladder.

LOOK TO THE PEOPLE WHO INSPIRE YOU OR THAT YOU'RE ADMIRING, PEOPLE WHO ARE GOING TO INFLUENCE HOW YOU MAKE DECISIONS—HOW YOU TALK, HOW YOU BEHAVE AT WORK... AND MIMIC WHAT THEY DO.

Time

Timing is one of the biggest things—because you can't give people time back. Customers may wait in lines that are 15-20 minutes to get to get to the window and place the order. But by the time they place their order, it's very imperative on our behalf, to make sure that that person is not waiting more than 7-minutes to *get* their order. I can give you money back. You can give me food back. We could throw that food away. You can always do that, but I don't have the ability to give you time back.

Space

We are limited on space on a truck; therefore everything has a place. We make sure that we always, always, always put everything in the exact same spot so it can be found by the next person.

Listening

We have to be listening and communicating on the truck in order for those orders to get out within less than 7 minutes of having placed the order. A lot of times, the customer will say, "Let me get a spicy chicken sandwich with fries." I recall that to the customer loud enough for the kitchen to listen, so the staff can go ahead and be working on your order, while I'm taking your payment. That's how we get it out the window fast. Most of the workers that have come on a truck, they pick up on that right away and they're like, "No [I have to] listen." If the guys in the back are joking, laughing, and talking and can't hear me as a cashier calling out the order—then we got a problem. So, everybody's got to turn their ears on. The person in the window communicating with the customer is the one who gets to talk really loudly. Everybody else has got to turn their volume down. Once they know that, they still actually have a really fun time working on the truck.

> **YOU HAVE TO REMEMBER EMPATHY BECAUSE WE DON'T KNOW EVERYONE. EVERYONE'S GOT A DIFFERENT BACKGROUND, A DIFFERENT EXPERIENCE, EVERY SINGLE ONE OF US. SO BE CAREFUL WE DON'T START MAKING ASSUMPTIONS.**

Repeat Order Loudly

We multitask. We're putting the order in at the same time the guest makes it and making sure that the guest understands what they're getting. I recall that [order] to the customer, but loud enough for the kitchen to listen, so the staff can go ahead and be working on your order, while I'm taking your payment. And that's how we get it out the window fast.

Volume Up

It's really important to project [your voice], choosing which words to use and to be able to communicate to the customer you're directing. At the same time [I'm talking with the customer], I'm talking loud enough for the people behind that person to hear too. I'll make sure I talk about it loud enough to where they can understand—that it connects with the people next in line. And then by the time they make it up to the window, "Oh yeah, I heard you tell that person not to get the medium because it's got three Peppers in there." And then we keep it moving, just move on to the next thing.

Everybody's Job

I've taught my workers how to pay attention to the bigger picture, so they don't get into that cycle of, "I don't want to do that. That's not my job. I don't go over there and do that because that's what he does." No, we all have to do this. We all have to pay attention. Then we can flow.

Career Advancement

I don't expect to keep a great worker forever. The ones that were excellent workers for me, I knew that I would lose them soon—that they were going to move on to the job that they're supposed to be working in or they were going to go off to college for a career their supposed to be studying for. If my place of employment can help get them out of the starting blocks and be that pathway to get into a career. I want to do that.

Empathy

Everybody comes from different backgrounds. Their home life, with conditioning, you know traumas and whatnot, the wins, and the losses that they've experienced. Everybody's gone through different funnels. Everybody. So, you can't treat everybody the same, right? You have to remember empathy because we don't know everyone. Everyone's got a different background, a different experience, every single one of us. So be careful we don't start making assumptions. In hospitality, empathy is the gift that we have to give people.

17

To-Go / Pickup

Phone Behavior, Delivery Drivers, and Making that 10-Second Guest Interaction Count

During the pandemic we saw one major element of food service completely change: the focus on delivery and pickup skyrocketed across our country. We were well on this track way before the pandemic hit, but this pushed us along much quicker. What didn't get pushed along as quickly was the customer service in this process and how can we continue to make the guest experience fantastic.

Pickups from delivery drivers can be challenging because you may have different drivers showing up who don't know how your system works. Try to be gracious and patient.

Most guests can order either through the restaurant website or through what are called third-party websites or apps. A few of the popular ones will sound familiar to you: Über Eats, Grubhub, DoorDash, etc. The guests will take care of the ordering themselves. A lot of guests prefer this method; it's quicker and easier, depending on their needs. If they are picking up, it means your window of interaction will be very brief. They have spent the same amount of money and possibly tipped, but you only have a ten-to-fifteen-second interaction when they come in to pick it up. While it's a brief interaction, a lot of things can get forgotten or taken for granted.

It's easy to ask someone their name or number and hand them a to-go bag. This is not the type of interaction that we want to get used to. We want to make that ten-to-fifteen-second interaction count. If they are picking up from the counter, check the bag, and verbally clarify their order with them. This isn't just to ensure no mistakes were made on the service side; it's a moment to present them with the order they are about to take home and enjoy. That positive energy must be there, the same way it is when we greet a guest and take their order. Take a brief moment to be present with the guest, ask them if they need anything else, thank them, and wish them a good day.

Pickups from delivery drivers can be challenging because you may have different drivers showing up who don't know how your system works. Try to be gracious and patient. It's not always the easiest relationship, but the fact is you are working with this other person to ensure the correct order gets to your guest. So, it's just as important that we have double-checked that order, guests' requests were honored, it's packaged correctly with the right utensils and condiments, and the food is hot and ready at the time that the third-party delivery person arrives for pickup.

YOUR PHONE BEHAVIOR SHOULD BE AS GRACIOUS AS IF THEY WERE STANDING IN FRONT OF YOU.

The phone call is where many communication errors occur in the process of someone ordering or trying to find out information about menu items. It's hard in a working restaurant that may be very loud, filled with people, with music in the background and interruptions occurring. This is the perfect recipe for a mistake to happen. Ensure you are speaking clearly enough that the caller can understand you. And a reminder: your place of business may be loud, but that does not mean that you must yell into the phone. The person on the other end is most likely not in a loud environment and should be able to hear you on their end. If you are unsure, you can always ask: "Can you hear me clearly?" "Would you like me to speak up?" Your phone behavior should be as gracious as if they were standing in front of you. "Do you have any questions about our menu items?" "What would you like to order?" "Is there anything else I may help you with?"

It's always odd to me when I'm on the phone ordering from a restaurant and they sound like I'm a huge pain because I called at a busy time. Most of the time, the guest on the phone is spending the same amount of money as they would if they dined in. They deserve your attention and graciousness. "Hold, OK!" is not a great way to answer the phone. It's not good phone etiquette to come back on the phone and yell, "Yeah, what do you want?" While your tone might be strained because you are hurried, busy, and juggling things to do, you need to treat the person on the phone as you would a guest standing in front of you.

WITH TECHNOLOGY CHANGING RAPIDLY, WE WILL SEE MANY ADJUSTMENTS TO HOW WE CAN GET FOOD TO OUR GUESTS IN A TIMELIER, GUEST-PREFERRED WAY. THE THING THAT WILL NOT CHANGE IS OUR ABILITY TO TREAT OUR TAKE-OUT AND TO-GO GUESTS WITH THE SAME CARE WE TREAT OUR DINE-IN GUESTS.

If someone is ordering on the phone, you want to ensure you are receiving the exact information they are giving you. Always repeat it back. You can never be sure where they may be calling from or what their reception is like, so clarifying an order is very important when taking the guest's order—just as you would clarify with a guest in front of you before you push the Send button to the kitchen. The fifteen seconds it takes to clarify the order is much easier to do than remaking an order after someone drives to your restaurant to pick up their order and it is wrong. And a lot easier than explaining to the kitchen why an order was put in incorrectly.

With technology changing rapidly, we will see many adjustments to how we can get food to our guests in a timelier, guest-preferred way. The thing that will not change is our ability to treat our take-out and to-go guests with the same care we treat our dine-in guests. If anything, we need to master that ten-to-fifteen-second interaction with them, so they feel valued and return to your business.

18

BRAD KENT

CO-FOUNDER - BLAZE PIZZA

I first experienced Brad Kent's delicious pizza at Olio Wood Fired pizza in Grand Central Market in Los Angeles. Blaze Pizza has become a nationally recognized Fast Casual pizza restaurant based on their incredible commitment to great ingredients, pizza, and their ability to connect with their guests.

Ingredients and Guests

Food is about a sharing experience. It's a huge part of our training. It's about guest services and explaining the ingredients to the staff so they can pass that on to the guest if they want that information. This is what burrata [cheese] is, this is where it is made, this is the company that makes it. We would do tastings of different burratas, just so people knew ours was the best tasting: the creamiest, the sweetest, the lightest.

We've had these kids that had never seen fresh mozzarella before, they didn't know what the differences were. And we were able to explain that to them. They are excited now about being a part of this. And that excitement translates to greater job satisfaction, great retention of employees; it also translates to your guests—because now we can explain to a guest when they ask, "What's the difference between this mozzarella and that mozzarella?" *This is whole milk and comes from Idaho, and this one comes from New York.*

Greeters and Acknowledgement

When you walk into a Blaze, you always want an order taker, the first person you see, to be the smiliest, friendliest, most outgoing person in the restaurant. That's your first experience as a guest. That's the first person that is going to say "Hello" to you. We train for that. Even if they are greeting someone and talking to them and someone else walks in, they are supposed to stop and acknowledge that person too.

Guest's Name

We put the guest's name on the paper liner because we want people to feel welcome. People like to hear their name. So, we can call out, "Hey Joe, welcome to Blaze. What kind of sauce would you like?" And we want our employees to use the guest's name three times while they walk down the line.

> WE WANT TO FOCUS THE ATTENTION ON THE GUEST EXPERIENCE. SO, THE FOOD SHOULD SPEAK FOR ITSELF; WE DON'T NEED PEOPLE TO BE LOOKING UP TOP. WE WANT OUR EMPLOYEES TALKING TO PEOPLE.

First-Time Guests

The very first thing we do when someone comes into Blaze, unless they are obvious regulars, is that we ask, "Is this your first time at Blaze?" And we write a little smiley face in the corner of their order paper, so everyone knows to give them a little extra attention. If it is their first time, we will walk them through the process—Blaze can be kind of complicated if you've never been to an assembly-line type of place and ushered though a line in two minutes to create your own pizza. It's a fast concept, and that is part of the brand. We want people to feel like they are taken care of, even though they are moving though the line quickly. By the time you pay, your pizza should be ready in a minute.

Interaction vs. the Boards

The [menu] boards are above the line. People aren't here to order food off a board, they are here to order food from you. We want to focus the attention on the guest experience. So, the food should speak for itself. We don't need [guests] to be looking up top [at the menu boards]. We want our employees talking to people, eye to eye, making that conversation, and asking them, "Which of these sauces would you like?" And that not only keeps the employee and guest connected, but it keeps the customer looking at the food, deciding what they want on their pizza and that also helps the line move faster. We are doing up to 200 transactions per hour.

ONCE THE GUEST SITS DOWN, SOMEONE SHOULD ADDRESS THEM WHILE THEY ARE SITTING DOWN IN OUR DINING ROOM. SOMEONE IS GOING TO COME BY THEIR TABLE WHILE THEY ARE EATING—AT LEAST ONCE—AND SAY, "HOW IS EVERYTHING GOING?

The Show

You are on display. You are part of the experience. Your uniform should be clean; you should have energy. Our colors are energetic; the sayings on our shirts are energetic because we want it to be visually interesting. So, people with tattoos, and piercings, that's really cool because that is part of our experience. People being themselves in our environment. If you want people to be themselves and you want them to be a part of the experience for the guest, this is all letting people express themselves. And that's going to create a very interesting experience for the guest. And how else can we make them part of the environment? I think this is one of the things that keeps people wanting to work here, because people can express themselves and be themselves. The protocol is that it must meet with the local standards of health officials. No droopy earrings, holes in their shirts, [ripped] jeans, open-toed shoes.

Follow Up in the Dining Room

Once the guest sits down, someone should address them while they are sitting down in our dining room. Someone is going to come by their table while they are eating—at least once—and say, "How is everything going? Can I get you another drink? Can I offer a refill? Can I get another napkin for you? Let me get that for you or let me get your trash for you." These are things that fast food doesn't do and things that casual dining does, but you usually have to leave a tip for it. It's something we don't expect a tip for; it's part of our value proposition. And if there is something wrong, you will know right then, and we can fix it.

19

THE RESET

TAKE A BREAK. TAKE A BREATH. IT'S A GAME OF ADJUSTMENTS.

My childhood soccer coach, Margaret Cunningham, taught me a valuable lesson when I started playing on her team in fourth grade. I didn't use it until many years later when I finally understood what she was talking about.

Mrs. Cunningham would use a technique to calm players down when we were getting rowdy or overwhelmed with the thrill of the sport. She would gather us around, and she would tell everyone to stop and breathe. "Take a big deep breath and blow it out slowly." And she would count back from five or ten. And we would relax. If a kid was having a meltdown, she would take them through this technique, and it worked.

Many years later, I was bartending at a bar in Hollywood. I was in the heat of the job, backed up, pouring drinks as fast as possible and dealing with unhappy guests. When alcohol is involved, customers can become aggressive, demanding, and even rude. My friend Gary, a seasoned pro behind the bar, told me early on, remember to take five. Go reset. If you don't, all of this will just build up and burn you out. I remembered Margaret Cunningham. I'd go outside, catch my breath, count backwards from five or ten and slowly match my breaths with it. It always helped relax me. Don't get me wrong, I wasn't floating back into work on a magic carpet, but it did ground me and allowed me to reset.

Being in hospitality and customer service can be exhausting. It's expected that we give a lot, and we must be open to receiving a lot, since we are front-facing. We get the opportunity to deal with a lot of amazing, engaging guests, but also some demanding, verbally aggressive guests. Sometimes people are just having a bad day, and we are on the receiving side of that energy. Some customers don't understand why we don't have something they want, can't comprehend that at times we make mistakes, or feel it is their job to treat us as someone who *must* do anything they tell us to do. It doesn't feel good when that energy is aimed at those of us trying to help them from across a counter.

WHATEVER HAPPENED TODAY OR TONIGHT STAYS THERE. TOMORROW, WE HAVE A CHANCE TO DO IT DIFFERENTLY. TOMORROW, WE HAVE A CHANCE TO BE BETTER.

The point is this: we can't do anything to change every person who walks in the door. We can, however, take a moment to keep ourselves in balance, adjust, and learn how we can ride the wave of customer interactions and service. You must take time to reset, even if it's just for one, two, or five minutes. Find a technique that grounds you. If you can't step away, maybe you can adjust your point of view in the moment. Often, if I was slammed at the bar, and it was a high-demand crowd, I'd simply envision the customers' hearts as giant, red, beating cartoon hearts. Like straight out of a Looney Tunes episode. Kooky? Sure. But it would help me get through a couple of tough hours. It helped me reframe my perspective. It was a reset, keeping me in touch with a little bit of humanity on a crazy Saturday night in Hollywood.

A phrase I think about is "Don't react, just take a breath." If something riles me up, I can take a moment, a breath, and then choose how I want to respond. This was a quick version of what Mrs. Cunningham taught me. I've been in some interactions with some very rude guests where I wanted to react immediately. Slowly, I learned, if I just take a long breath, it will help me create a pause. That's it! And in that moment I created, I didn't engage right away, and was able to take some space and assess the situation. This ability to take a pause made a huge difference in my ability to be of true service even in the most challenging situations. It took practice to get used to, but it makes a huge difference in all aspects of my life.

One of my favorite things about working in hospitality is that tomorrow is a new day. Whatever happened today or tonight stays there. Tomorrow, we have a chance to do it differently. Tomorrow, we have a chance to be better. Tomorrow, we have a chance to *have a better time* doing our jobs. You see this reset in sports. It's not about the bad play or the mistake. It's about how you deal with that mistake. That is what defines the great players, the ones who are able to adjust in the moment and continue to contribute to the team. In restaurants, it's not about a bad day or night of service, it's about how we are able to rebound, learn, adapt, come back, and adjust the next day.

20

MELISSA KARAFF

--·--◈·❖·◈--·--

DISTRICT MANAGER - STARBUCKS

I met Melissa through a friend, and she just amazes me with how much she loves the people she works with—her team. She is passionate about how to engage guests even during a quick coffee experience. Her spirit is refreshing and inspiring.

Interviews

I get [interviewees] talking, and I want personality. I'm looking for a smile, and I love it when they have done some research. One of my questions is: "When you go into a Starbucks, what do you like?" If they say something like, "I like the service and the friendliness,"—because that's a big part—or "I like the one I go to near my house because they know my name, and I like the caramel macchiato, and they know that and how I like mine"—that's good to me because they know that that is an expectation. It's kind of amazing how many people apply for a job here that have never been to a Starbucks. They've never been in, never got anything, don't know what the drinks are.

One of my questions is: Tell me about a time you got in trouble at work, a time when you did something wrong? How they dealt with that situation and their feeling on it afterwards is what I'm looking for. *I made a mistake and now I have to fix it.*

I want people to be comfortable in the interview. But sometimes they are too relaxed. They swear or talk really bad about past employers. Sometimes I don't need to know all the details of why you didn't like your last manager and why you left the job. "She was always telling me what to do!" Well, I will be the person telling you what to do, because that's how it works. You will always have a boss, and that boss will always have expectations of you, and that is part of having a job.

High School Experience

I look for commitments. This one applicant didn't have a lot of work experience, so she had to use school as her experience. Clubs she was a part of—it shows you can lead and how you have been led. Situations where they have had to do extra activities, build relationships. A community service thing says a lot because they are doing something outside of their normal. Theater groups are great because they have worked as a team, put on a production, dealt with stress, memorized lines. And all those things can be used for this job. i.e., I have a great memory, I can remember recipes. Sports are good—they have worked as a team, have received criticism, changed direction to make something better, taken feedback, and made something better.

Commitment

What is your commitment? We have Partners (employees) that come in and are so excited to learn everything. They ask questions and are excited to learn. The other person is the person that doesn't care and isn't there. Not grasping the idea, but more importantly not *caring* enough to grasp onto the idea. This might be a part-time job on someone's road to what they really want to do, but I look for what their commitment to us is. I've had a lot of great Partners who have come in and have their life goals, but they understand they need to make money until they achieve those larger goals. I think Starbucks is flexible, but you need to fully be here when you are supposed to.

Consistency

Coffee knowledge doesn't mean they are going to be the best fit for Starbucks. We follow strict recipes. This isn't a spot to make your drink however you think it should be. You need to grasp specific recipes and embrace consistency, because our customers want the same vanilla recipe at this store as at a store 100 miles away. That is Starbucks—you can count on the same recipe and drink every time.

Customization

Starbucks customers like customization. They can come in and change up their item. It's a great way to increase an average ticket. Do you want another shot in here? Do you want to try other things than lattes? You are helping your average ticket, but you are also helping the guest experience. And they may remember that and come back because that customer likes your recommendations.

> WE DO THE DISHES, CLEAN THE BATHROOMS, MOP THE
> FLOORS, MAKE THE MOCHAS. IT'S EVERYTHING. NOT JUST
> MAKING DRINKS AND SMILING.

Training

Usually [new employees have] eight hours [of] computer training—computer and video that gets them used to the layout and solidify ideas. Two weeks with the barista trainer—learning drips, pour-overs, making espresso drinks, frappes, working on register and the lobby. We do give people breakdowns of the recipes for them to look at. The bases of the recipes are the same, so you can make most of the drinks, or know the base.

Taking Direction When Slammed

It can't always be hugs and flowers. In the rush or dinner service, you have to check your expectations. Communication might be shorter when we are slammed. People might be a little shorter when communicating in those intense situations, but it doesn't mean they are mad. They just might not have the time to ask in that sweet way. I want to hire people that can take that direction too.

Speed

Fast and friendly—how can you be both? Keep it nice, but you have to keep the line moving. If you know their drink, you can get it started and save time. We do eighty to a hundred orders per thirty minutes.

The Full Picture

We do the dishes, clean the bathrooms, mop the floors, make the mochas. It's everything. Not just making drinks and smiling. People sometimes don't see all of it. You have to do it all. I'm a store manager and I have to clean the bathrooms as well.

21

GOODBYE

FINISHING THE GUEST EXPERIENCE STRONG

Working behind the counter and in restaurants for many years, I've noticed one element of the guest interaction is forgotten more than anything: Goodbye. It gets missed for many reasons and at the worst possible time. A cashier greets their guest at the counter, says good morning, assists the guest with understanding the menu, explains a few dishes, puts the whole order in, give the guest a receipt or stand with a number, asks the guest to swipe their card through the credit card holder, guest is prompted to tip or not, guest picks a percentage of tip, pushes OK. The cashier asks if they would like a receipt, hopefully the cashier thanks the guest, and informs them of the expected wait time for their order. They then immediately turn to the next person in line and say, "Next."

But we missed the goodbye. It follows the thank-you. "Have a good evening, see you soon." "Enjoy your afternoon." "Have a great weekend!" These are ways you can say goodbye. I used to call it "the fumble on the goal line." Unfortunately, I've watched lots of tables get up from an experience in a coffee shop, casual restaurant, even fine dining, and walk all the way from their table to the door with no one saying anything to them. People forget the goodbye a lot.

When you say thank you, that is for the guest paying for the services and products that you provided. When you say goodbye, you are wishing them a good rest of their day. These are two separate things. They usually follow each other quickly, but you should be aware that they both need to happen with a guest who has chosen to come into your business and buy something. Any business, I think, but certainly in a hospitality business. Sometimes I have gotten neither a thank-you nor goodbye, and my likelihood of returning is slim. If I get one, I'm happy. But if someone does both and they really mean it, it's a great way to end an interaction. And I will almost always return if I enjoyed the product as well.

THE GUEST EXPERIENCE ISN'T DONE UNTIL THEY HAVE WALKED OUT YOUR DOOR. TRY TO ENSURE YOU CAN CONNECT ONE LAST TIME BEFORE THEY LEAVE.

It's a weird feeling we don't want to give to anyone. We all know what it's like to leave a party or an event without someone saying goodbye to us. It just feels off. Unless you are trying to sneak out of the place unnoticed. My buddy Josh Goldman used to say, "Have you ever let a guest leave your house without saying goodbye? No. That would be weird. We don't do that, so why would we forget to do it in our restaurants?"

The guest experience isn't done until they have walked out your door. Try to ensure you can connect one last time before they leave. I know it can be difficult with staffing issues and busy parts of the day. While you may not have a chance to say goodbye to all guests, don't allow it to become a regular thing. The risk in counter service establishments is that employees think the interaction is done as soon as the guest leaves the counter. This is not true. The more often you can touch base with a guest about how they are enjoying their drinks or meals, and certainly wish them a good evening, the more likely they are to return. Great service brings people back, and saying goodbye to your guests is great service.

22

THOM CROSBY

PRESIDENT - PAL'S SUDDEN SERVICE

Thom Crosby is the owner of the award-winning Pal's Sudden Service, fast food restaurants found in Tennessee and throughout the south. Pal's Sudden Service was one the first Fast Food restaurants in the country to win the Malcolm Baldridge National Quality Award, the nation's highest Presidential honor for performance excellence through innovation, improvement, and visionary leadership.

Greeting the Guest

Our service standards are: Always be present and never let a customer come up to an order station and have to wait. (So always be at your station. Immediately make eye contact, smile, lean forward toward the customer, toward their space; be peppy and upbeat in your talk and conversation.) We have very succinct steps on each one of those things.

We are always on the positive, and we want an energetic, pleasant farewell. In our area, you always hear people say, "Have a good one." That causes the hair on the back of my neck to stand up. "Have a good one?" Have a good what? You have to be detailed about it. If you want to say have something good, say "Have a good afternoon," or "Have a good evening," or "Have a good rest of your morning." We think it's important for you to show respect of others.

Career Skills

We try to relate to our employees that there are certain aspects that we are working with you on, that you will be able to leverage for the rest of your life, no matter what career you chase. If you follow a few of these key things we are laying out in front of you, you will excel where maybe others [won't]. Communication and how you express yourself is one of those things.

YOU WILL BE TOMORROW WHAT YOU TO PRACTICE TODAY.

We spend a lot of time talking to [employees] about [how] you are who you are: "You will be tomorrow what you practice today." We try to set up a scenario where they see it. Are you going into a medical career? An engineering career? Or the military? These are forms of communication that we are asking you to practice, and I guarantee you, whether you are going to be a worker or a leader, going into another industry, the more effective [a] communicator you are—the higher and quicker you are going to achieve the success you to want, no matter what your career is. If you can get this down pat, you are going to excel in the future. You will be tomorrow what you practice today. And your personality will shine through all of this.

Authenticity

We are dealing with two pieces of authenticity. The brand's authenticity and then you as a distinct individual, your authenticity. And we want to marry the two together. We tell our employees: here are our standards, especially with service and behavior; here is an upper and lower limit; here's the standard range—you can bounce around in between those points anywhere you want to.

Accepting Feedback and Criticism

Are you getting criticism from the customer, and how are you receiving that? And are you getting criticism from a peer or a leader inside the company, and how are you receiving that? We are constantly talking to people about problems—we call them *opportunities* to put a positive spin on it. The customer (or leader or peer) cares enough about us to point out where there is an opportunity for us to improve. They are giving us the gift of feedback, and we need to be appreciative of that.

Internal Customers

We train people on how to answer, "Who is your customer?" The ultimate customer is the paying customer, but my internal customer is the sandwich maker. One of the aspects we have set up culturally is that there is a "supplier–customer" relationship in our company between every employee. And our mission states that we are going to "delight all customers in a way that creates loyalty"—and that means internal customers too. And so, we've set up this positive mindset—you are my customer internally—and that starts resonating with the way that they are going to communicate with those internal customers, right back to the way that we are going to hold them to the same high standard on the ultimate paying customer.

Job-Jumping

If you switch jobs too frequently, you may have multiple learnings where you are only skimming the surface—it's not deep dives. And if you are going to become a true and valuable asset, especially as you're moving into the future, the deeper dive you do, the more thoroughly you understand a concept, the things that drive the concept, and the things that really drive results. Then you will have the ability to take what you know and go replicate it.

Certification

We have the training technology, [and] the training methods to get any employee that comes into the company to make 100 on their graduation. Graduation isn't the end-all, be-all to us. Certification trumps graduation. What the real world wants is—what can you do and repeat time after time? What level can you do that at, time after time? How can you capture a curveball and hit it? Every time it's thrown, [you] hit it! And nothing's getting by you. You are doing it in the real world and replicating it time after time after time.

Calibration

We have a strong belief that people, like machines, go out of calibration. Like when you have to have your car tuned up. All humans go out of calibration; I go out of calibration. We have an electronic system that has all of the employees in it, with an algorithm that tells us if it's time to blank out your ability to work on that station—you are no longer considered trained or certified on this specific station—you can no longer work this station or be assigned to that station until you have been reverified and are reentered into the system. Then you are certified again to work that station. To make this work with 1,200 employees, we are recertifying people on stations every day of the year. It's just reverification that everyone understands that they know how to achieve that top standard all the time. And our commitment to that even applies to me—the CEO. Everyone in the company goes through recertification! We have this big net that will catch us and get us back on standard.

On the risk of putting in this huge effort of training employees and then possibly having them leave:

What if I don't, and they stay?

23

DENISE RODRIGUEZ

HOSPITALITY PROFESSIONAL - NEW YORK CITY

I met Denise at NY Pizzeria Suprema, when she walked up and offered a kind hello and wanted to make sure I was having a great experience enjoying my slice of pizza. I was! NY Pizza Suprema is one of the city's most popular pizza spots, across the street from Madison Square Garden. Denise has worked throughout the city in a variety of areas of hospitality.

Shoes

First thing you want to do is to make sure that you have supportive shoes. You know black sneakers, rubber sole, something cushioned, with an arch. Because you're going to be standing on your feet for a long period of time. You don't want to slip and fall. So, we always tell people, make sure that you have sneakers with a rubber sole. And black shoes are preferred: as they look more clean, more sophisticated.

The Love

When I was young, I was in the food business. I tried food because it was fast-paced, it was active, it was nice. You meet people from all sorts of places.

I enjoyed it. I love talking with people, I love talking with customers and with guests. You have to take the time if you want to help somebody. Let it come from your heart and help the people with joy. I love making them feel welcome, making them feel loved, because I like to be treated that way.

> PEOPLE ARE HAVING HARD LIVES. DON'T GIVE THEM GRIEF BECAUSE YOU HAVE NO IDEA WHAT THEY'RE GOING THROUGH, WHAT KIND OF DAY OR KIND OF LIFE THEY ARE LIVING. BE NICE, BE COURTEOUS, BE KIND. TURN IT AROUND.

Ask Questions

When I worked in a bagel store in Brooklyn, I used to love hiring people that didn't have experience—if they were curious. I'd see something in them and say, "This is the kind of person you want to mold, this is the kind of person you want to train, you want to lift up. You want them to grow within the company." They ask questions. If you just go to a job and you don't ask questions and you're not motivated—you're not going to learn anything.

Turn It Around

When I trained my staff many years ago, in a deli in the West Village, we had customers that came in and some of them were very difficult people. I would say to my crew, "You know what, turn it around. Don't put your mentality with them. Turn it around because you don't know what goes on behind doors. People are having hard lives. Don't give them grief because you have no idea what they're going through, what kind of day or kind of life they are living. Be nice, be courteous, be kind. Turn it around. Yes, they come in with a face, they come in with the attitude, they bark at us. Turn it around. Greet them nicely. Complement them."

Great Work Environments

If you work in a toxic environment, the negativity is going to spread. If you work in a great environment, where everybody is on the same level, everybody's cheering, they're dedicated, they love what they're doing—it's like medicine. You work together well, you know what I mean? You go into work and it's, "Good morning. How are you doing?" You're feeling good. We joke around in between AND we get the work done. Then customers come with, "Hey, how you doing? Good morning! I love you!" You have that vibe, and it feels great because everybody's on the same level. It's like everybody's feeling good and positive. Everybody's keeping their negative nonsense and BS on outside [of work] and that's exactly what you need to do.

Running Low on items

[Running out of items because you haven't communicated to management that you are low] is frustrating, and it messes up your whole energy. You have to care in order to communicate. Caring is the only way you're going to go to the manager or whoever is doing the orderings and say, "By the way, listen, we are low on such and such." You have to make sure you have it, never be in doubt. You have to communicate. It's all about communicate, communicate, communicate. You have to find out [what you are running low on] because if you don't—not only is it bad for the company and bad for that person that's not communicating, but it's bad for the customer.

The most important thing in the world [for a business] is word of mouth, so if you're constantly telling customers, "Oh, we don't have this. I'm sorry we don't have that." The customer will say that place is ridiculous, I'm not going there anymore. So, you lose that customer, you lose the sale, and your reputation.

Sucks, right? When you find out at the last minute that you don't have it, well there's really nothing you can do. So, communication is a big thing. I've seen this happen in so many different places and it's just a simple word. Communicate.

Knowing Local Events

Having a calendar of the shows and the performances of everybody who is going to be at The Garden is a big plus. It's right behind us, so everyone is aware. It's a big help because that sets us up. We know what's going on so that we could be ready. The counter servers, they're aware of what's going on, so they're able to be like, "Oh, the Knicks are playing the Celtics." Or whatever the event is. They're able to kind of have a conversation with customers, right there.

Enthusiasm to Learn

To be open to new things is sometimes the most important thing. If I like the way you work, I like the way you interact with others, I like your spirit, I like your teamwork, that's great! But if somebody starts their new job and they don't have that and they don't have an open mind, they don't bring that enthusiasm to get in there and learn and want to grow and make that job work, then it's not going to work out. They have to have that enthusiasm.

24

My Boss/My Friend

Navigating Changing Roles and Friendships

One of my favorite things about working in hospitality is how quickly friendships develop. I'm certain that it happens because we work together in quick-paced, team-driven environments and we have to depend on each other. There must be a lot of communication and understanding, and relationships develop in a very short amount of time. So, work relationships can be rapidly layered with new friendships. It's awesome. It's how I've made some of the best friends in my life.

However, that layering of work relationships and friendships can sometimes cause some friction. Early on in my time in restaurants and bars, I had to learn one lesson a few times. Since I quickly became friends with the people I worked with, I fell into the trap of forgetting my boss was my boss, and I would just look at our relationship as a friendship. This happened with direct supervisors and managers. At times I became a little too casual regarding their direction and feedback, and this led to some hard but excellent learning moments for me.

A friend who I had known casually offered me a job at her company in the events department. She was one of the leaders of the division, and they needed a fill-in bartender for their catering staff. I happily took the gig. On my very first day I saw her walking with some people as we were setting up a party for a few hundred people. I yelled out, "Hey Laura! What's up?!!" I got a nice nod, but a quizzical look.

Another bartender said, "You know she's walking through with the head of LA Kings; this is his party tonight." I quickly realized, while she might be my friend and I had a friend relationship with her outside of work, this required a different type of communication. It was a different set of roles for us.

SINCE I QUICKLY BECAME FRIENDS WITH THE PEOPLE I WORKED WITH, I FELL INTO THE TRAP OF FORGETTING MY BOSS WAS MY BOSS, AND I WOULD JUST LOOK AT OUR RELATIONSHIP AS A FRIENDSHIP.

Another learning opportunity came when I had been bartending for a few years at a place in Hollywood. My manager, who had become my friend in the four years since he had hired me, asked if he could talk with me. He asked me if things were OK. He noticed I had lost my very friendly vibe at the bar and thought I was starting to seem a little annoyed with guests, not as focused.

I was really annoyed that he said these things. I told him, "I thought you were my friend."

He said, "I am your friend, but I also run this business, and I must make sure we are doing what's best for the business. I'm your manager here first." It took a while for me to understand where he was coming from. In retrospect, it was one of the best and most honest things a manager has ever said to me.

This is a lesson I've learned over and over, and each time it became much easier. Through many years in this business, I have learned how to balance my working relationships with my friend relationships. I like working with people I enjoy, becoming friends with my co-workers and leaders. But it has helped me—and I hope it helps you—to understand that our supervisors and managers have a job to do and that we need to respect that relationship with them. Ultimately, we must make sure the business needs are met and that we are always working as a team to accomplish our goals.

We may become friends with our bosses, or our friends may become our bosses. Relationships at work will change, and our work dynamics will shift. It's part of working with a team for a while. If you remain open to change and support your co-workers in their new roles, you will have a much better transition than if you aren't aware of the support they need from you. And hopefully, the same will happen with your co-workers when you get a promotion and your work responsibilities shift.

BE OPEN TO NEW LEADERSHIP AND DIRECTION FROM PEOPLE WHO ARE NOW TAKING ON MORE RESPONSIBILITY. YOUR FRIENDS' SUCCESSES ARE NOT YOUR FAILURES.

I had an experience where I started working at a job with a friend, and I was promoted to supervisor quickly, and he kept making jokes at our shift line-ups and goofing around when I was supposed to be leading the team. We had kidded around a lot when I wasn't in a supervisor position. It was a hard transition for both of us. I didn't want to "pull rank" or anything like that, but at a certain point I took him aside and I told him I needed his support. "You keep undercutting me and joking around when I tell the team we need to do something." I was surprised. He told me he totally understood. And we were cool from then on. He eventually became the manager of the whole place!

There will be shifts in the roles in the places you work. Try to remember to be supportive of those promotions. Be open to new leadership and direction from people who are now taking on more responsibility. Your friends' successes are not your failures. They're an opportunity for you to support them and make the needs of the business your priority when you are at work.

25

CHARLES BABINSKI

————◦◦◦◦◦————

CO-FOUNDER - GO GET EM TIGER

My wife introduced me to Go Get Em Tiger because she loves both their Los Feliz and Highland Park locations. Having visited both many times now, I discovered that the service is outstanding and the coffee is amazing. Charles Babinski is a Co-founder of this Los Angeles hot spot.

Hiring

I've always had a three-prong kind of test that served really well. Number one: are they kind? Generally speaking, if you get a sense that somebody is a kind person who wants to take care of other people, that's just the foundation. Them acting on their own volition will generally yield good results. And them acting as an agent of the company will yield good results. Where those two things intersect and where they diverge is always a larger conversation, but kindness is of paramount importance.

Second, do they know what the job is? I think specialty coffee is actually a place where there's this disconnect—a lot of people think that their job at a fancy coffee shop is going to be tasting coffee and talking about the flavors and telling a story of a farmer. Realistically, a lot of the job is cleaning, organizing, hustling to get things done. Everybody wants to give flavor descriptors, and no one wants to clean the toilets when they overflow. And there is a kind of rhythm, a reality of coffee-shop service that we would always try to pin down in the interview: Do you know what it's like? Do you know what you're in for?

Third, are they willing to do that job? I would say that every time we hired somebody who hit all three of those, they were a good employee, and it was a worthwhile hire. And every time an employee didn't work out, or there [was] something drastically wrong with the fit, [it] could usually be tied down to one of those three issues.

Work of the Day

It's service: You're talking to people, handling people's issues, handling the complications that come up throughout the day. I think what people associate with specialty coffee work is really the 5% after you have satisfactorily done the other 95% of coffee-shop work. Obviously, that 5% is incredibly consequential, and it's really important, and it's what defines us, but the way that you get to that is by doing the other stuff well.

We really considered ourselves first and foremost a service-centric business, and that was always the top value and the most important thing. Meeting customers' needs, meeting customers where they were, acting with kindness—even with difficult customer interactions—all that stuff is super-important. The idea that this *is* the work! You're going to get a wave of people who are going to be interacting with you *before* they've had their coffee for the day and, you know, you have to be ready for it. The most respected in business and in the shop are the ones who [are] able to execute those values at a high level.

Trust

You know, the amount of people who are trying to take advantage of you is pretty small—most people's problems are real problems, so trusting the customer to be honest is also a completely reasonable thing to do. Most big, sort of Chernobyl-level bad customer interactions are aggravated or bounded on some distrust along the chain: the barista doesn't trust the customer, the manager doesn't trust the barista, the barista doesn't trust themselves. When all that stuff is on the level—problems become a lot easier to solve.

> **WE REALLY CONSIDERED OURSELVES FIRST AND FOREMOST A SERVICE-CENTRIC BUSINESS, AND THAT WAS ALWAYS THE TOP VALUE AND THE MOST IMPORTANT THING. MEETING CUSTOMERS' NEEDS, MEETING CUSTOMERS WHERE THEY WERE, ACTING WITH KINDNESS.**

Coffee Shop as a Touchpoint

We talk explicitly about a coffee shop being a really meaningful touchpoint for people discovering the neighborhood or discovering a city, and that was always considered good service, to be able to provide that. At our shop [G&B Coffee] in Grand Central Market [in Los Angeles], we would talk explicitly about wanting to be kind of the concierge desk of downtown. We'd get a million questions about Angels Flight [an old railway attraction] or various downtown things. And you'd pick it up through osmosis. That's the goal! You want to be able to suggest restaurants, you want to be able to suggest places to go, you want to say, "Hey, check out this cool thing!" Along with being able to tell people where the bathrooms are or where the subway is and all that. One hundred percent, that's the coolest thing. That's one of the best things about coffee shops—you go to a new city, you find a coffee shop and just start asking questions. In my opinion, they will tend to be the most clued in of any service professional.

Service

At a coffee shop doing good service, you're motivated by a level of discipline and a level of empathy that is always present. It's not going to turn on or off depending on somebody giving you money. I think that's great, and I really have an extraordinary amount of respect for the service professionals in coffee in the United States and other countries. There's a level and a respect for service that is really high here and is growing and worth investing in, because it's a meaningful skill, a very consequential skill. If you're somebody who is interacting with people on a daily basis, and you are providing this meaningful touchpoint with discipline, skill, and understanding of your community—that's a person who's making their community better: a better place to live, a better place to interact with other people, find more opportunities, live a more meaningful life—it's a small thing, but it adds up. Coffee shops are all about just small, meaningful things that add up over the course of months and years. If you can serve people and meet them on that level, and be that part of a community... you will have success.

26

SAFETY

—⋅⊰✦⊱⋅—

TAKING TIME AND PAYING ATTENTION TO SAFETY

I've chopped off the tip of my thumb, thrown my back out, pulled a lateral muscle moving a stack of chairs, worn wrist and arm braces hidden under shirts, soaked my feet in a tub after work, and so on. Stress on body parts happens, injuries occur, and accidents can happen in any job. I've done some dumb things, and I've developed some good routines for self-care. I used to think, it's part of the job—any restaurant job. But most of this was quite preventable. Safety is one of those things that's very easy to forget about when we're spending a lot of time engaging with guests or customers. You can easily get sidetracked. In this business, we spend a lot of time multitasking—performing a task while talking to a guest or coworkers—and in those interactions, we can forget the proper way to do tasks or precautions we need to make before we do something.

A Few Tips

First off, shoes. Rubber-soled shoes. I've gotten used to this, having worked in and around food for a long time, but I recently visited a kitchen in dress shoes (leather soles) and almost fell on my butt. Rubber-soled, non-slip, comfortable, supportive shoes are essential for safety and working on your feet all day long.

I love someone who hustles. It's a great quality. But you need to think about some important precautions to take when you are moving quickly, lifting, or carrying anything. Safety first! The biggest gift you can give yourself is the assessment moment. Just stop! Think for a moment: Is this the safest way to do this? If you give yourself that moment, you will have prevented most situations just because of your awareness of the risk. There is a reason there is proper technique in every training video I've seen—but assessing what you are going to be carrying first is the key to the next right step. Is this the safest way? Can you do it yourself, or do you need someone to help you?

As comfortable as you may get around knives and chopping food, you need to respect them. I chopped off just the very tip of my thumb—it grew back, though. I was quite surprised at how quickly it grew back. And this was after I took a free knife skills course from an awesome chef I worked with. Pay attention. I got comfortable, cocky, and distracted. And when you take your eyes off the task, accidents happen. Always use the correct methods when chopping and preparing food. Clean your cutlery and store it safely.

> **JUST STOP! THINK FOR A MOMENT: IS THIS THE SAFEST WAY TO DO THIS? IF YOU GIVE YOURSELF THAT MOMENT, YOU WILL HAVE PREVENTED MOST SITUATIONS JUST BECAUSE OF YOUR AWARENESS OF THE RISK.**

Don't be embarrassed to have a little support. I tended bar for a long time and started to have stress in my right forearm. The repetitive motion of pouring would make my right forearm ache in the later part of my shift. I started with a brace that tightened around the tendon, and it did wonders for the incessant ache. Eventually I started to use my left hand and arm as much as I used my right. Being right-handed, I had been favoring my right, but once I started training my left, I was able to switch it up, and eventually I didn't need the brace. I was able to balance the stress by switching my pouring arms.

Clean floors! Be aware. Look around and *down*! If you work with liquids or with food, the likelihood that you could slip on something is high. So, the first way is to work wisely and safely, and don't spill anything. We already talked about safe shoes, but the more you get used to watching where you walk and anticipating problem areas, the better off you will be. Also, pick it up and clean it up. It may not be your spill or error on the ground, but the sooner it is dealt with, the safer our work environment becomes for everyone.

Be careful when you are moving containers back and forth from the walk-ins or refrigerators. Often, condensation can build up on the bottom of the container, and you may not notice it slowly dripping as you walk across the floor. You can give a quick wipe of the bottom before you move it but scan the floor to make sure you haven't accidentally caused a safety hazard.

IF YOU SEE A MESS, PICK IT UP. BE PROACTIVE.

I'm always surprised when I walk into the restroom of most restaurants and see the mess people leave. I don't know the handwashing habits of the men in restaurants, but often it looks like someone took a bath in the sink and left water all over the counter. I'm amazed at this feat. While I don't understand, out of habit from working in restaurants, I must clean the water off the counter and tidy up before I leave.

I've worked in many places where it was the policy to make sure you pick up the bathroom after you use it. Meaning, if you see some paper towels on the floor, pick them up and put them in the trash. If the trash looks like it's overflowing, take it outside and dump it. In the case of the sink, I wipe it down and throw the towels in the trash. After I have done this quick pickup, I wash my hands thoroughly and exit.

The reason I'm shocked when I walk into restaurant bathrooms is it's clear to me that most people who work there do not clean up the bathroom after they use it.

It just falls on the person who is scheduled to clean it, if that process even exists. This is just one of those things you must accept in hospitality: If you see a mess, pick it up. Be proactive. Most guests will use your restroom if they need to, so it should be as clean as the dining area. I know people who avoid restaurants because no one details the restroom. Don't assume the next person will do it; just pick up what you can to keep it clean.

27

VIVIAN KU

---◦◦◦---

CHEF/OWNER - PINE AND CRANE, JOY

I fell in love with Joy and Pine & Crane along with everyone else who waits eagerly in line for their amazing food. Vivian Ku prizes her staff, who are attentive and upbeat. She shared some insights with me on how it all works.

The Long Line

We try to let people know how the line works. We're constantly thinking of ways to save more time and make it easier for guests where we can. Sometimes people wait in line for so long and once they reach the counter, that's our only interaction with the guest. So, we make their experience worthwhile, and how we do that is to make sure that we are patient with guests. We take our time to explain the menu. We never rush guests, making sure we are mindful with each guest. It becomes a lot less overwhelming and a lot of that is focusing on great hospitality, mindful hospitality.

Working with Third-Party Food Delivery Services

That is tricky to manage because in some ways they're a continuation of ourselves, [Third-Party food delivery couriers] are helping us serve our guests. We have no control over who delivers the food. We don't hire the couriers, obviously. But I think it's recognizing that we'll probably get further if we all work together. A lot of them are just trying to do the best that they can, and sometimes they are frustrated because there might be a delay. We actually have shared goals-they just want to make the delivery quickly and securely as possible, and so I think trying to remember that is important.

WE WANT TO MAKE SURE WE'RE NOT JUST TREATING OUR GUESTS WELL, WE'RE TREATING EACH OTHER WELL.

Sometimes, someone has to sort of set the tone in terms of how we want that relationship to go. We're in the hospitality industry, and we want to make sure we're not just treating our guests well, we're treating each other well, in terms of the team itself—and then also that should extend to the couriers. But just as with guests and with our own co-workers, I think people have bad days, and in this industry we're kind of called on to sometimes give people the benefit of doubt, and once you do that, it goes a really long way. Be the bigger person in some ways, and oftentimes you will see their mood change, and then all of a sudden you form a relationship. We know a lot of our couriers by name now.

Dropping Food and Checking Back

I always remind our team that ordering at the register is great. It's super-efficient. People pay up front, so as a result, we serve more guests per table than we would in fine dining or full service. But to keep in mind that because of that, we don't have the opportunity to quality-check all of the time, and we don't have one server per table, so if someone doesn't like something, there's not a lot of opportunity to find out. In traditional settings, you could ask how things are and have one person do a glance-over, at least.

**WE WANT TO MAKE SURE THAT THE INTERACTIONS DON'T
JUST END ONCE WE'RE DONE DROPPING OFF THE FOOD.
WHEN YOU'RE ONE OF THE SERVERS ON THE FLOOR, YOU'RE
CONSTANTLY TAKING STOCK OF HOW QUICKLY PEOPLE ARE
EATING. WHAT'S THE DYNAMIC? WHAT'S THE SITUATION?**

Here, everyone has to be extra mindful—so if you observe that someone doesn't touch a dish, you want to jump in there before the end of the meal. There's more of a likelihood that someone [is] not going to like something and sneak out, and we wouldn't know about it. We want to make sure that the interactions don't just end once we're done dropping off the food. When you're one of the servers on the floor, you're constantly taking stock of how quickly people are eating. *What's the dynamic? What's the situation?* If you walk around and you notice everyone else in the party is making progress, and this is one person is making very slow progress, it's probably time to check in with them and see. I think that only comes from being mindful, realizing this seems off, this person's expression is off. So, the challenge is, how do you make time to be mindful, observe those details, when you're also running around trying to make five trips within three minutes?

28

Omar Anani

Chef/Restaurateur - Saffron De Twah, The Twisted Mitten Food Truck

Omar Anani is the Chef owner of Saffron De Twah in Detroit, Michigan. He is a 2-time James Beard finalist for Best Chef in the Great Lakes region as well as Chopped Champion Great American Showdown: North.

Food and Stories

When we run a restaurant, it's all about guest experience. Because at the end of the day- they can get food from anywhere. People don't buy what you do, they buy why you do it. That story makes you connected with the food in some way, shape, or form and food is all about stories creating memories.

Prepared to Interview

Come in prepared to interview. You're interviewing for a job, right? So don't come in wearing flip flops and pajama pants. That's not a way to interview. I am looking for people that want to work at my restaurant. They should know about the restaurant's history. All it takes is a couple keyword searches, so utilize the technology that's at your disposal. I can tell you what year the company was formed, I can tell you who the owner is, I can find articles. Come in prepared to ask questions because somebody who has questions, to me, is engaged. I'm like, "Do you really want to work here? Why do you want to work here? What questions do you have?" So do your research. Know who you're going to work for. Come prepared for an interview. Do that work because that's going to make you more desirable.

> COME IN PREPARED TO ASK QUESTIONS BECAUSE
> SOMEBODY WHO HAS QUESTIONS, TO ME, IS ENGAGED. I'M
> LIKE, "DO YOU REALLY WANT TO WORK HERE? WHY DO
> YOU WANT TO WORK HERE? WHAT QUESTIONS DO YOU
> HAVE?" SO DO YOUR RESEARCH.

Hospitality Mindset

It's all about the mindset. I think it takes a certain type of person to be in our industry. Sometimes we are going to be dealing with people who are angry, upset, or ungrateful, and it's our job to turn that around. We never know what they're going through. We don't know what kind of day they're having, but we do have opportunities to make their day better.

Repeating the Order

It's confirming that things are right before you take the guest's money. Repeating the order to them. Getting a verbal yes or no, not just a head nod. If the order is really big say, "Hey, I just want to make sure we got this." And then, go over it again with them. It's the attention to details.

Investing in Yourself

If you want to be a leader, you have to invest in yourself. Regardless of what you're doing in life, whether it's as a cook, as a chef, as a server, you have to invest in yourself. If you're not investing in yourself, if you're not saying "Hey, I need some leadership classes. Hey, I don't even know how to read a [Profit and Loss Report]. Someone teach me!" These are the things that you have to be able to do to be successful. You can't expect someone to just give it to you. You have to go out and get it for yourself.

> **YOUR JOB IS TO ATTRACT PEOPLE AND SELL THINGS. SELL SOME MORE THINGS AND MANAGE THEIR EXPERIENCE. MAKE SURE THEY WANT MORE AND THEY COME BACK. IT'S ALL THESE THINGS PUT TOGETHER, CREATING AN EXPERIENCE.**

Take Time

Taking the time to explain an item to a guest is going to benefit you tenfold because, here's the thing: the amount of money it cost acquire a new guest is way higher than the amount of money it would cost for you to take a minute to explain something to that guest, creating a regular. I'll give you a prime example. I worked the counter this last weekend. Usually, our least selling appetizer on the list has always been the Loaded Hummus. At the end of the weekend, the [employees] go, "Chef, what's up? You just made hummus the number one selling appetizer in the restaurant over the weekend. How did you do that?" I was like, "How do you guys sell the loaded hummus?" They said, "Well you know, it' Hummus. Everyone knows what Hummus is. We didn't really have to sell it."

I said, OK, let me tell you how I explain what I say when I sell the hummus to them and why they bought it.

"So, let me tell you something about our Loaded Hummus: Our hummus is made from scratch, we soaked our chickpeas overnight. It's cooked. The loaded portion of it is absolutely amazing - the set changes seasonally. Right now, it is olive tapenade, tomatoes, cucumbers, toasted almond salsas, walnuts, Aleppo pepper, sumac, citrus, olive oil that we make in the house, and your choice of pita chips or bread." When you make it sound that delicious, the customer is like, "Oh, let me try the hummus too!" No matter what they ordered before that, they're going to be like, "I know we ordered a lot, but you've got to throw that one on there too!" That's your job as the counter person.

World of Wrestling

Here's what people don't get about [your job as a counter service person: your job is not to sit there and take orders. Your job is not to sell food. You are basically Vince McMahon! Vince McMahon, you know the owner of the WWE. Your job is to create an experience. Think about professional wrestlers: they've got to come out on stage, be flamboyant, be extroverted, do this dog and pony show. Put butts in seats and sell some [merchandise]. All that is kind of like a service person's job. You are the entire world wrestling organization. Your job is to attract people and sell things. Sell some more things and manage their experience. Make sure they want more and they come back. It's all these things put together, creating an experience. And it's a front counter person who's supposed to do all of this. In under a minute.

Take-out Window

The takeout person's job is to make the experience as hospitable as possible. When I worked Fast Food, one of my first jobs was at Burger King. One of the measures of our Quality of Service, was Speed of Service. I learned really quickly working that window that there was one simple way to get people off of my pad 10 times faster. It's all about the details and asking simple questions. Usually when people would pull up to the Front window [after they place their order at the Back window] the person at the Front window would say, "Hey, can I get you a straw? Can I get you some ketchup? Napkins? Sauces?"

So, when I was at the back window, taking the order, I made sure to figure out what sauces and items they wanted while I was there, so the person at the Front window could just make sure everything was in the bag. That employee would only have to open up their customer's bag and verify: "You've got a Double cheeseburger meal, extra-large fries, Diet Coke, two ketchup packets, and an apple pie." Just repeat the order to them, confirm that it's what they ordered, hand them their bag and they drive off without even opening it. I just saved 10 seconds on my Speed of Service. That all came from training.

29

TIME TO BOUNCE

WHEN YOU MAY HAVE TO LEAVE
YOUR JOB

For most of us, there will come a time when it is time for you to leave the place you work. I use the word *bounce* because my friend used to tell me, "It's time for me to bounce, these people just got crazy!" He had a history of leaving jobs quickly. Not a great track record.

I've seen people bounce for a few reasons: not being happy with their job role, not being happy with their co-workers, not being happy with their boss. Whether you're an employee or a manager, I encourage you to do your best to communicate and see if you can find a way to stay at the place you work. Many great companies I've had the honor of working with have a massive priority to work with the employee and have them stay. A lot of these situations come out of helping two people work together to find a solution or helping a manager and employee find a better way to communicate.

I've bounced from most of my jobs for one reason or another. While I'm proud to say I have never been fired, there was one departure that came close. When I was eighteen, I was given the ultimatum to help a sanitation company clean out hundreds of port-a-potties on a blazing hot day at a Winston Cup track in Sonoma. This had not been in my scope of work at that job that summer. I gave it a go and had to leave work within the first couple of hours. I quit the next day.

This was also the only time I've never given a two-week notice when leaving a job. My dad was so mad I didn't give them a two-week notice. So, I had to go in and apologize to the owners the next day. I offered to work the two weeks, but they declined. It was a good lesson for me to learn early on. Regardless of the reason, try your best to give your company a two-week notice if you are planning to bounce. This is the courtesy anyone who takes a chance on you deserves.

The Role

You may come to a place where you are unhappy in your current role. You don't feel challenged by your job, you'd like more responsibility, or you just don't have that enthusiastic feeling about this job anymore. These things all make sense. When you are feeling these things, it's a good opportunity to talk with your manager about getting excited about the job again or taking on a different position. The position might not be open at the time, but at least you've started a discussion and expressed that you want to learn more. While things don't always happen overnight, be patient. After you've exhausted all options and you still feel it's not a right fit, then it may be time to bounce.

Your Co-workers

You may find you have been working with the same people too long, need a change, or are frustrated at how some of the people on the team treat you. Hopefully you can communicate well with them or your manager and find a way to improve that working relationship. Always give yourself time to get to know the people you work with, especially if you are new. It does take some time to find a good rhythm with people. Some of my best friends from working in hospitality are people I butted heads with when we first worked together. But if you have tried the best you can to improve your work relationships and feel like you have no options left...you may need to bounce. I had an aggressive boss once who told someone, "That's just the way it is here; if you don't like, I don't know what to tell you." That's a green light. To bounce.

TRY YOUR BEST TO GIVE YOUR COMPANY A TWO-WEEK NOTICE IF YOU ARE PLANNING TO BOUNCE.

Passive Aggression

My least favorite form of bad communication is passive-aggressive behavior that is behind a fake façade of charm and hospitality: undercutting remarks and direction that are aimed at making you always feel like you aren't good enough for your position. This falls well short of constructive feedback and genuine direction. It can create an US and THEM divide among co-workers, and it never gets to the root of the issue. People often resort to passive aggressive behavior when they are unhappy but don't feel empowered to do anything about it. If you are feeling frustrated or don't have the tools to communicate directly, reach out to a mentor or manager you think is good at direct communication and seek their advice.

Always try to be direct; don't continue to make these types of side comments to anyone you work with. It really undercuts your relationships and a company's goal to have a healthy constructive environment. If you have a manager or leader who uses this type of behavior to motivate the team, you may want to have a direct conversation with them to understand the root of the issues they are having with your job performance. I've seen a lot of people leave jobs because of the incessant passive-aggressive behavior in the workplace culture. Poor communication doesn't make people feel good.

A Toxic Boss

Hospitality can be very stressful at times, people can be rude to each other, and miscommunications can happen in the heat of a shift. A healthy place understands that while this may happen on occasion, it should never be the norm. In the best places I've worked, we have been able to apologize for our shortness during a hectic shift as well as remind each other of the great job we did after a rough shift. As I've mentioned before, this is a learning environment, all the time. We are always receiving feedback and growing. But there is a line that our bosses and guests can easily cross. Two older common practices that are unacceptable:

- A good leader doesn't need to scream at you. If you are subject to that type of behavior from anyone on a regular basis and it is not changing, you may want to seek other job opportunities.

- If your boss thinks it's OK to let guests yell at you, you should have a serious conversation about the need for leadership to support you in those situations. There is never a moment when a guest should be allowed to yell at an employee without a manager coming to that employee's aid. A guest can complain and disagree, but if it crosses a line and you don't feel supported in your role, you may want to seek other job opportunities.

30

KEN SCHILLER

———◦✦◦———

PRESIDENT - K&N MANAGEMENT

K&N management is the owner of Mighty Fine Burgers, Fries and Shakes as well as the licensed area developer of the four Austin, Texas area locations of Rudy's Country Store & Bar-B-Q. K&N Management is a winner of the Malcolm Baldrige National Quality Award, the nation's highest Presidential honor for performance excellence through innovation, improvement, and visionary leadership.

Interviews

It's determining if [the job candidates] align with our core values and our cultural stuff—if they are a nice, smiling, personable type of individual. They are actually being scored as soon as enter the front door by our receptionist. We are very intentional and very thorough about our interview process. But it's not experience or skillset-based.

Reading the Customer

We don't expect [our employees] to be robots and have them quote a verbatim script. We train them to read each [guest]: Is the guest in a hurry? Looking down at their cellphone? Want to get in and out with correct service? Or is the guest more casual and want to talk and play a little bit? [Employees] are taught to read each guest and tailor their approach accordingly.

Feedback

We provide a lot of feedback. We don't frame it as criticism. But we measure everything in the business. We do this thing we call 'game film', where individuals come in with hidden cameras and pose as customers and they record their entire transaction. Then the team members that were involved view the film and score themselves, and then we score them. It's kind of like a sports team that watches game film after their game. They are looking for what they did right: Were there any gaps? If somebody doesn't embrace feedback and measures, and [they] aren't a cultural fit, then our opinion is "A Players [that is, players on the A team] want to be measured because it validates they are an A Player." It's the low performers that fear measures.

Job-Jumping

One, I don't think you learn as much and develop as fast as you can by jumping around, because you are always in training and trying to learn a new culture and finding your place instead of being able to focus on improving skill sets, competency, and forming relationships within an organization. Second, it's just not going to look good to employers that see that you've been jumping around. History is the best predictor of the future. They may assume you are going to jump from them also. I just see it as a lose-lose.

Advancement

You are given opportunities to advance and learn leadership. We do some in-house leadership training. I think it's important to teach someone the difference between management and leadership. They are both important, but very different. You are only going to go as far as your leadership takes you. We consider, for example, our trainers in the restaurants, most of [whom] are hourly employees that started as cashiers, as one of the most critical positions in the company. Because that is who is interacting with and training the people that are going to serve and delight our guests.

Delivering Food to the Table

We do deliver to the table. When the guest leaves the register, they are given a table tracker. There are GPS locators underneath our tables, and we are able to know where that guest is sitting. So, our runners are able to deliver the food right to the guest without having to call out a name or look for a number on the table. Each person has their own bag with their name on it, and the runner makes sure that the bag goes to the right person

31

ABUSE AND TOXICITY

RECOGNIZING AWFUL PEOPLE AND DANGEROUS WORKPLACES

I've worked in some challenging environments where verbal abuse and harassment were tolerated. There are all types of businesses with owners who don't appreciate their employees, don't understand the law, rule with abusive behavior, or stand idly by allowing that type of behavior to occur. One would think that a restaurant—whose business it is to exude good standards of hospitality—would treat their employees well, but sadly, that is not always the case.

I know a lot has changed in the hospitality environment in recent years, and I'm happy to see that the toxic environments that existed before are being addressed, challenged, and changed. More owners and managers are finding healthy ways to communicate and ensure their employees are working in emotionally and physically safe environments. They are protecting their employees from abusive guests and creating better ways of communication to improve discussions around toxic work situations. They understand that their turnover rates are lower and productivity is higher when their employees feel safe in their workplace.

Verbal Abuse

For years I thought it was normal to work in an environment where it was OK to get screamed at. It's been a while since I experienced that type of behavior, and I'm glad it's being addressed in our industry. Having worked with many managers and leaders, I know there is a much more productive route to getting what you want than raising your voice, calling associates names, or ever using physical abuse as motivation.

A TOXIC ENVIRONMENT IS CREATED BY CONTINUOUS BAD BEHAVIOR AND NO ONE SAYING ANYTHING.

And honestly, I've allowed abusive verbal behavior to continue and appear normal by not speaking up. I remember as a server, standing there with my co-workers, thinking, "Well, at least my boss isn't yelling at *me* this time." And keeping my head down as a co-worker gets yelled at. I never raised my voice. There is always a time and a place to speak up. Even if it's not in that direct moment, when tensions may be high, it's good to tell your manager. If you don't feel satisfied with how that is handled, you should take it to your human resources department or owner of the company immediately.

Harassment

When I worked as a barback in Hollywood, before I became a bartender, I had to wade through a packed room of people with a bus tub over my head, filled with dirty glasses. There were a lot of hands being placed and grabbing where they shouldn't. I just sort of got used to occasional groping. I didn't want to complain, be seen as uncool, or admit it bothered me. But it did. And I didn't say anything. If I had said something, I'm positive I would have been supported by the owner and staff there. But I chose not to say anything. You don't always have a supportive manager in bars where there are a bunch of young patrons and a vibrant party atmosphere. Some owners won't do anything about this for their servers in these situations. They encourage the servers to be more tolerant of handsy guests. This is not normal!

Verbal and sexual harassment can come from co-workers, owners, vendors, and guests. It's important to know that you have rights, and anytime you feel uncomfortable you should say something. If you voice a concern where you feel abused, bullied, or in danger, it is not appropriate for someone to say to you, "It's no big deal," "Don't worry about it," "It's just the way it is here." You should take your concern to a manager, and if you don't feel it is addressed, go up the ladder to their boss, Human Resources, or the owner.

Toxicity

A toxic environment is created by continuous bad behavior and no one saying anything. People may be afraid of retaliation, so they continue to stay quiet. That was my case in certain situations where I didn't want to be reassigned to worse shifts or lose them altogether. A toxic environment can be a place where bullying exists, gossip is prevalent, cliques of certain workers harass others or management is ineffective and using these tactics themselves. You can try to surround yourself with supportive co-workers in this type of situation, but if it's a persistent environment, you should talk to management, HR, or owners to address the issues more directly. I now understand that by not speaking up and just simply leaving a company, I still allowed that behavior to continue and go unchallenged in my absence.

Danger

Without the support of good leadership, you may find yourself in a dangerous work environment. Not just emotionally dangerous, but physically. That could be from aggressive and threatening customers, co-workers, or a work environment where safety standards are continuously ignored. If sexual harassment is prevalent, that is an abusive and dangerous situation that needs to be addressed. You are legally protected in many cases, but again, the fear of retaliation causes a lot of people to stay silent. If you find that HR and ownership are not addressing these issues, you can either leave, seek legal assistance, or do both.

IF A WORK ENVIRONMENT IS DANGEROUS, TOXIC, OR ABUSIVE, YOUR FIRST RESPONSIBILITY IS TO PROTECT YOURSELF.

If a work environment is dangerous, toxic, or abusive, your first responsibility is to protect yourself. Hopefully you can instigate part of the solution by communicating with management, HR, and owners to improve these areas at work. If not, you may need to leave. I've made the decision to leave a job before I had another and learned that wasn't always the best decision. On a couple of occasions, I was jobless for more than a few months, and it became pretty stressful without an income. After that, I always made sure I secured another job before I left one. If you have the time, try to secure a job before you leave your current job.

We have come a long way in improving work environments, and my hope is that in any situation that is uncomfortable, you are able to talk with your management about it. That they will address the issues and improve your work environment. When these problems continue on, with no one talking about them out of fear or retaliation or harm, the environment just continues to grow worse. Nothing happens. And a culture of abuse, toxicity, and danger is allowed to continue.

32

Maggie Castaneda

━━⋐◆⋑━━

Managing Partner - Don Pedro Carnitas

Maggie helps operate her famous family-owned restaurant that's been a part of the Pilsen neighborhood of Chicago for over 30-years. With returning guests, lots of regulars, and long lines, she shared some of her thoughts on service.

Communicating with People in Line

I'll walk through the line, and I'll let them know we're in between batches right now. "They are pulling out the next [batch of carnitas]!" As long as there is communication between the people that are working here and the people that are waiting to buy our food, the customer is ok. When there's no communication, that is when people can get upset and you can get a little bit of hostility. "It's taking too long!" I think that's just normal with anybody if they're hungry, right? Reassurance is a big thing. [The customer] needs to get some positive reinforcement, some reassurance from the people that work here. We have to make sure we are making eye contact or touching base with them. You always want to look at them straight in the face. It's when you don't communicate, that people become a little irate, or they feel like no one cares about them.

**IT'S GREAT TO SEE SOMEONE COME OUT OF THEIR SHELL
AND FLOURISH AT WHAT THEY DO. AND THEN, THEY
ACTUALLY LOVE WHAT THEY DO.**

Keep the Line Moving

I always tell [our cashiers], "O.k., you already know what we sell, it's not a big menu, but you don't want to get too far into the explanation, unless it's somebody that's completely new to us. Keep it simple. 'What are you looking for? How much do you need? And what do you like? If there's any extras that you want: tortillas, onions, cilantro, limes -just let us know.'" Keep it simple. Our cashiers are priceless to us because they can determine how fast the line goes.

Happy and Welcome

You've got to be happy. I'm all about making myself happy and making other people happy these days. You know what? People come in, and I want them to feel like they're coming to their family's house to eat. It just feels good when you're somewhere, and they make you feel welcome.

Out of their Shell

All of the people that I have working, the younger people, are pretty outgoing. I do have one [employee] who was super shy, and it took us a while to have her master that. Sometimes, when she was coming up to somebody, she seemed a little shy. I told her, [talk with the guests] little by little, until you feel comfortable, you know? You actually get to see them kind of learn this whole thing and come out of their shell.

She's comfortable with her job now, and she's just great at it! It's always a "Good morning!" a "Good afternoon, how can I help you?" And that's her way of getting her foot in the door with the customers. It's great to see someone come out of their shell and flourish at what they do. And then, they actually love what they do. When I see someone accelerate at doing something that they're enjoying, that's fantastic. What else can I ask for? And that's something that we've instilled in them, we encourage them to be better, to do better. If [management's] not better and we're not doing it right, they're not going to want to do it right.

The Customer

The customer comes first. That is our boss. I always let them know that the customer that's coming in, that's buying from us, that's our boss. That's my boss. That's your boss. Without them, we're not here.

Agitated Customers

I always let our employees know that [mean customers] are not a reflection on them. They should never take it personally. Just let it roll off your back. Forget it. If you let that stuff bother you, you're going to become the person that's being mean, and you don't want that! It's a reflection of who they are, you know. Let that go!

IF YOU'RE GOING TO DO IT, DO IT TO THE BEST OF YOUR ABILITY. BECAUSE THAT'LL SHOW PEOPLE WHO YOU REALLY ARE AT YOUR CORE.

Low on Items

I have my rule of thumb; Everybody should know where we're at with everything. If you feel like there's something running low, let me know. Nine times out of ten, I've already caught it and I've already ordered it. But I'm human and I make mistakes. So, I always need a third, fourth or fifth pair of eyes. I'll always make a checklist for myself, *and* I'll just ask randomly, "Hey, do we have everything we need today?" There will always be one or two people that will say, "You know what? Let me just double check because I'm not sure." That's when we catch something. It's just a good way to get people to double check what we have and what we need to do.

Be Your Best

Do the best you can at everything that you're going to do in life. Whether it's [being] a cashier, a lawyer, a server, a doctor, a barista. If you're going to do it, do it to the best of your ability. Because that'll show people who you really are at your core. And don't sweat the small stuff. There are bigger things in life to worry about.

33

GARY CHAU

---❖❖❖---

CO-FOUNDER - CAFFE LUXXE

Caffe Luxxe consists of 7 award-winning, upscale coffee cafes and a roastery throughout Los Angeles. The attention to detail and upscale counter service experience has created a massive following of dedicated regulars.

Vibe

The first thing you experience when you come in, in terms of our ambition, is a complete sensorial experience. How does the place look? What's the music that you hear? What are the other sounds (espresso machine, ambiance, etc.)? The most important part of this experience is that we have great people. In our business, people are the most important elements of this experience. Our business is about people. Coffee just happens to be the mechanical part of it to draw people in. But at the end of the day, we're more about people and relationships.

Finding Information

That first question is important: "What do you like?" That's how the interaction needs to start, as opposed to me putting my [favorite] thing on the guest first. That is always a red flag. Another key question would be, "What do you normally drink?" And that will help guide us to steer someone towards a specific type of drink. For example, "Oh, I always like milk in my coffee." And we would steer them towards perhaps espresso-based drinks that have milk: such as a latte or cappuccino. We ask them, "What type of flavor do you usually enjoy your coffee?" or we might even ask them, "What are you currently drinking?" These questions give us some hints as to what they enjoy. For example, if someone is interested in dark chocolate, and a bold, classic flavor profile, we most likely won't recommend a light, roasted coffee, black, because that will be more of a fruity citrus. A more acidic experience that they're not expecting.

PEOPLE ARE THE MOST IMPORTANT ELEMENTS OF THIS EXPERIENCE. OUR BUSINESS IS ABOUT PEOPLE.

Skills

Because we do have a fairly young team base, and sometimes it may actually be their very first job, an important skill is how to work with other people. We tend to prefer someone that has the right attitude, the right curiosity, the right positive outlook on life. And someone who we know we can shape into a graceful employee. We have people who may not have worked with or collaborated with others in a team environment before, so I think that kind of skill is learned—which they may not realize or appreciate until later on in life.

Collaboration

I learned how to communicate with strangers and how to help people by asking them the right questions. I also learned how to work with people who are my peers, at all different levels, and it didn't really matter whether that person was my boss or a brand-new trainee. I learned how to work with all kinds of people and collaborate together for the same goal that we're all trying to achieve. To me, that is an important people skill that I hope [employees] learn and appreciate and take with them for the rest of their lives. And that doesn't have anything to do with working in a coffee shop.

THE HIGHER THE PRICE, THE HIGHER THE EXPECTATION. THE HIGHER THE PRICE, THE MORE CURIOUS THE CUSTOMER IS GOING TO BE: "WHY IS THIS AT THAT PRICE?" OUR EMPLOYEES SHOULD KNOW THE ANSWER.

Knowledge

I think in in any kind of environment where a high price is being asked – the higher the price, the higher the expectation. The higher the price, the more curious the customer is going to be: "Why is this at that price?" Our employees should know the answer. The expectation from the customer is very detailed, and the explanation of this type of product is very important, especially when the customer can pull out their phone and look everything up. We need to be the shortcut to that. This is also a way to create a moment to have a conversation and get to know each other.

I'm not saying our coffee is at that level [of] extreme, but we're offering luxury high-end products, besides our coffee. So, the expectation is, if we're selling a bottle of $40 balsamic vinegar, a customer will likely come in and ask us detailed questions about it. They are more curious. "Why is this $40?" So, the answer from us cannot be something so simple, like, "It just tastes really good." It has to be about the extensive details and perhaps the top three to five key selling points of what makes that product special. This helps our customer justify that purchase in their mind...all of these things to be able to guide someone to the right purchase decision.

Multitasking

Everyone is actually multitasking, so we don't necessarily have a specific person who just runs the cash register. As part of someone's training, they will all start at a barback level, and that's so they can learn the base level of our operation and the operational needs in terms of cleaning, making sure that things are where they are, assisting the senior staff, [assisting] baristas with making drink orders, and prepping drinks for them. There's no one, for example, who just stands at the cash register and rings people up. We have a lot of respect for the restaurant business, and we learn a lot from our restaurant friends. The one thing here that's important to us is that we work as a collaborative team, and you have to understand what your position and your role is and how each member contributes to that team environment. That's one of the most important things for us, so that's why people multitask on the bar.

Cleaning

Our perspective: as you grow, go up the ranks, your responsibilities don't become less because of seniority—they become more. As you grow, you do more work because you don't forget where you came from, and [you] continue to share your responsibilities of everything you learned from when you first started as a barback. So, in my mind, everyone is the same and we all share in the workload. Just because you are more senior or doing a different role, everyone is bussing the tables, doing dishes, [helping] to clean the café.

And we have to remind people, "Hey, why is the barback the only one cleaning tables and you're just standing behind the bar? We are all responsible here. We are a team!" And their eyes light up, "Oh yeah, right." When we're busy, we know our assigned roles and specializations, so that way we can all collectively work efficiently together. But when there's downtime, we're all in this together—let's share the work on whatever needs to be done in order to reset ourselves for the next rush of people.

Business

We teach our employees basic business skills about how you operate and run a business in a profitable manner. That obviously depends on how high you decide to work with us and the level of skills that we teach you. I think people will learn that business is not easy, it's hard, and so we're training them on the basic fundamentals and opening their eyes as well. "Gosh, this isn't just some place where I swing coffee and then I go home. It's a place where I start to open my eyes and see that this is an operation and a business where I'm helping them hopefully make some money, so that we can all share and this. And this experience is something I can learn from and add to my skill set as I move on to other things in my life."

EVERYONE IS THE SAME AND WE ALL SHARE IN THE WORKLOAD. JUST BECAUSE YOU ARE MORE SENIOR OR DOING A DIFFERENT ROLE, EVERYONE IS BUSSING THE TABLES, DOING DISHES, [HELPING] TO CLEAN THE CAFÉ.

Co-Worker to Supervisor

In an environment where you see and interact with someone every single day, it's not hard to become friends because you're always chitchatting, socializing, or hanging out after work. I think in a coffee-shop environment, we create the sense of friendship amongst our customers and our staff. So, we will become friends with our customers and most certainly our co-workers.

The challenge is that when you become this co-worker/friend's supervisor and the two of you used to go to movies, dinners, whatever, you may feel a little awkward when you have to actually tell this person what to do. Those uncomfortable moments where you may need to correct them or even write them up for something are all new responsibilities that have shifted and may affect your relationship. It's hard because you're dealing with people you have become emotionally connected to, and now, all of a sudden, it becomes really difficult because this new relationship is not what you are used to.

It's OK to be friendly with each other, but there are scenarios where you cannot be friends because you're now the boss. And you're going to have to take those tough areas of responsibilities and need to help us manage our business in the right way.

One thing that we try to reinforce to help people visualize the difference is: It's OK to be friendly with each other, but there are scenarios where you cannot be friends because you're now the boss. And you're going to have to take those tough areas of responsibilities and need to help us manage our business in the right way. And you have to be professional about it. So, we have to teach our newly promoted supervisors and managers how to specifically deal with those kinds of tough conversations and situations. It's really about sitting down and going through a lesson plan of how to communicate in the right way with their staff.

Afterword

As I mentioned at the beginning, I hope this book inspires you to ask how you can be of service to others, improve what you are doing, innovate, and exceed your guests' expectations. The idea for this book started while I was working in a restaurant with others, trying to figure how we could make our guests' experience better each and every day. It's not rocket science. It starts with you wanting to connect with your guests, ask the right questions, and make sure they leave feeling happy with the intention of returning.

I thank you for reading this book, and I hope it inspires you to have some great conversations with your co-workers, leaders, employees, and managers. I'm grateful to all of those in this book who took the time to talk with me. I hope their words inspired you as much as they continue to inspire me and that you can come back to this book as you need it, finding answers to the questions we ask ourselves every day in hospitality.

How to Get Hired

Everything you need to know on Day 1

Now that you know what the options are, how do you get a job? What should you know before you walk through the door? The easiest way to see if the company is hiring is to check online. Go to the company website and look under Careers, or check out the multiple career sites online: Indeed.com, Careers.com, Glassdoor.com, Monster.com, etc. These will assist you in finding that specific job you want to apply for.

Do you apply online, or do you drop a résumé off at the specific store you want to be hired at? Both. If you drop by, you do not want to do it while they are very busy. Pick your time when it might be a little slow (not during the breakfast, lunch, or dinner rush—in between), and someone might be able to answer some questions. This also demonstrates some understanding of their business.

If you are going in to inquire about a job, you should look below at the Arrival and Dress sections, as they apply to anytime you walk into a business looking for a job. First impressions are important. You don't want to walk into a place that has a "Help Wanted" ad in the window in a tank top, unshaven, sweaty from your bike ride, and say, "Hey, I saw you were looking to hire someone and thought I'd stop and grab an application." Just keep enjoying your bike ride past the place. Go home, shower, change, come back, and walk through the door. It's going to increase your odds.

When you come back, be aware, they may tell you they only accept applications online; then you can inquire for information about their website. You may want to ask, "Are you hiring right now?" "Is the manager here?" "When is the best time to drop off a résumé to a manager?" Be quick and thoughtful, knowing that they are in the middle of serving guests.

Phone Interview

This can be common if the restaurant receives a high volume of applicants. They may decide to choose to do a phone interview, ask you some questions and get a feel for you before they decide to have you come in.

If you are informed via email or text that they want to talk to you at a certain time: BE PREPARED at that time. Find yourself a quiet space you can sit in, where you won't be distracted by any other sounds. Have a piece of paper and a pen (I always have two handy in case one runs out). This allows you to write down anything they may ask you to wear, bring, or prepare in the sit-down interview. Maybe you have a great memory—maybe you can hear well on a crowded bus or write notes while you drive (not recommended!)—but you are better off finding a quiet place where you and the interviewer can hear each other clearly and you can write down the correct information you need.

Phone Energy

Be careful that you have the same type of energy you would in an interview as you do on the phone. By this, I mean remain upbeat when talking on the phone, make sure you are speaking clearly, and listening well. Don't sit on a deep couch or lie down in a bed the way you might if you were talking to a friend. That will lessen your energy. A great trick is to smile while you talk on the phone. Sure, no one can see you, but you will be amazed at the positive energy this will give to the person on the receiving end.

Who's Talking?

Make sure you write down the name of the person calling you. This will come in handy should you meet with them in person. It also might be an assistant manager calling and conducting a prep interview for the second meeting with the manager. These are two names you should write down and remember, as you may need to reference them in your sit-down interview.

Early

Being on time to me means being ten minutes early. It's respectful and shows that you are serious about the job. So be prepared for that phone call before it comes in. If the call doesn't come in at the exact time, or even if it comes in ten minutes after the appointment, try not to get annoyed or irritated. Restaurants, as you will learn, are all about the needs of the guest. The manager or assistant manager may have had a guest to attend to or something unanticipated come up. Try to keep that in mind and stay positive, as you wait for the call.

Details

If you are given a time and a place to meet for the in-person interview or follow-up phone call, make sure you write it down properly and double-check it with the person you are talking to. Address, phone number, cross street. This shows that you are thorough and clarifies the exact information you need to make the next step in getting the job. Oh...and don't lose the piece of paper. I usually write a backup in my phone notes program or my phone's calendar.

Interview

When entering any interview, you should come in happy to be there. I hope you are. You should be upbeat, happy, with positive energy and an excitement for the job. If you love poke, great. If you think Chipotle is the best Mexican food you've ever had, great. If you only drink coffee from this specific place because it's awesome, well, that is awesome. That excitement is going to translate in your interview and ultimately to the guest who you will be serving. A smart manager will see that. If you don't have experience with serving food, don't worry. They will train you. Your energy and general understanding of what the job is about is the most important thing at this point.

Arrival

Remember—ten minutes early! Some of these places are very small and don't have a lot of tables. Usually, someone will tell you where to wait until a manager can come talk with you. Have a seat and wait patiently. It's a working restaurant, so be prepared to wait a while; things happen, and the manager might not be able to be with you immediately. You might want to ask for a menu as you wait. This allows you to familiarize yourself with it (if you haven't already gone online to look at it—I highly recommend this!)

Résumé

Bring two. Even if you already submitted it online, don't assume they will have a copy available. One could get smudged, or you may need them both in case two people are interviewing you.

Application

Some places will require that you fill out an application while you wait. You may be thinking: Well, why the heck did I go to all the trouble of typing out this résumé when you were just going to have me write it all down? Short answer: They need a copy for their records. The upside is that if your résumé is up to date, you will have all the pertinent information ready to copy onto the application.

Note: Make sure you have *all* your information, including old employer addresses and contact information. This information is not always printed on your résumé, so make sure you have it easily accessible. You don't want to be the person telling them you will get back to them with the information. Someone else could have their application completed and get the job because you weren't prepared. (By the way, I only know this because I learned the hard way. Be prepared!) An incomplete application makes you look unprepared, and you want to leave a positive first impression.

Dress

Someone told me once to dress in the style of the place you are applying. To play it safe, I would wear a collared shirt with some pants. Nice, clean jeans or slacks. Nice casual dress shoes or very nice sneakers. Showing up clean is the first step in that. Showered, smelling nice—but don't overdo it with the cologne or perfume. People want to smell food, not someone's perfume or cologne.

Waiting

As you wait, you may be tempted to go to your phone. Who of us doesn't when we are waiting? If you are going to look at your phone, maybe read about their menu online, look at their Instagram photos if they have them, look at something that is relative to what you are going to be talking about. It's keeping your head in the game. Think of it as a pregame warmup. If they have a printed menu, you can always look at one of those as you wait. Anything you do once you walk in the door should have to do with why you are there in the first place: to get a job.

History

Know about the place you are applying to. You don't have to have the history of the place memorized, but know something about it. Be familiar with their menu and the type of food they serve. If they specialize in items like Blizzards at DQ, know that. If they are known for their famous Double Double "Animal Style," like at In-N-Out, know about that. You are preparing to work for them. If you know something about their business and the products you are going to be selling, even before you walk in the door, you will be a step ahead of the competition.

Questions

There is some really good "Interview" advice from different managers and owners within this book. Many different questions could come your way, depending on who is conducting the interview and what their style is. They most likely will want to know about your past experiences of working with guests, co-workers, and managers. They may ask you about hobbies or school, especially if you don't have much work experience and this is a first job for you—they may just be trying to see how you have interacted with people in other aspects of your life. Try to be in the moment and answer honestly. They are just getting a feel for who you are. It's important. You are going to be the face of their company engaging with the guests; they want to know if you are the right fit for them.

Here are a couple of examples of interview questions. There are many different options online as well. I always find it good to have someone at home or a friend ask me some practice questions before my interview. That way I feel like I'm a little warmed up.

- **If you were hired, how long would you like to work here?**

"Five months" is not a good answer. People are looking for longevity. Employers want to invest in you and have you as a great employee for a long time. They understand if you are looking for a job for a year, as you finish school or pursue another interest. It's important to be honest. If you are applying for a seasonal job and you are interested in returning year after year, you might want to suggest you are interested in returning for seasonal employment. This way you are still demonstrating a long-term commitment within the constraints of your schedule.

- **What do you want to do/be in five years?**

If you can see how this job might help you in any aspect of achieving that goal, let them know that (e.g., I think serving different types of people daily and working with co-workers as a team is going to help me when I get my teaching credential).

- **Have you worked a job where you've helped prepare the dishes before?**

Having a positive take on an additional task that you haven't been exposed to might sound something like, "It would be great to learn about different preparations. I've always been curious about the intricacies of food and service and thought this might be a great intro."

The following questions might be asked of you if you have had prior work experience. **These are not trick questions**; the person hiring you wants to gauge your attitude and ability to adjust to situations that arise at work.

- **Give me an example of how you handled a difficult situation?**

- **Give me an example of how you helped a fellow co-worker?**

- **Give me an example where you helped a customer, and they were happy afterwards?**

Rehearse It: Role Play

In my many years of food service, the best teams I've ever been a part of worked on their skills. When waiting tables, we would practice for 10-minutes before guests arrived on role-playing different aspects of service. A few examples to use in counter service could be:

- **Walking up to the table (your co-workers pretending to be guests at the table) and checking in with the table "How are you enjoying your double cheeseburger? May I get you a refill on your Iced-T?"**

- **Getting quizzed by guests (your co-workers pretending to be the guest standing at the counter) asking how dishes are prepared or what the ingredients are in certain dishes.**

- **Getting quizzed by guests (your co-workers pretending to be the guest standing at the counter) on what ingredients are in certain coffee drinks or if other items have allergens.**

Role playing and rehearsing is an important way to work out the kinks, to be prepared. No matter how good you are at your job, it's a great brush up before you start a shift. It also keeps everyone on point with knowing the menu items. If you have a willing friend or family member, rehearse your interview for your job. Have them ask you the questions above or any other ones that are appropriate. Have them add some questions you don't expect. You never know what the questions will be, but a little rehearsal a least warms you up and gets you used to answering some unexpected questions. The point isn't to memorize the answers, it's to engage in an exercise that will prepare you for your interview.

Into Action: Use this Book Today

Here is a list of a few simple ways you could use this book to improve service for yourself or for your teams. The first rule is: keep it simple. Also, keep it to the point and short. I intentionally kept the chapters brief to facilitate this.

- Read through the book and highlight areas you want to improve. Make a list and slowly and intentionally focus on one topic at a time as you deal with guests.

- Find a topic in the book that you want to improve your skills on and read through that topic with a co-worker, supervisor, or friend. Discuss what it means to the two of you and how you could improve that aspect of service.

- If you are having a tough time focusing at work or getting into the work mindset, pick one small anecdote that you like in the book and read it a couple of times before your shift. Ask yourself how you can improve the guest experience around this. Sometimes one simple objective can move you into working with intention and focus.

- Read the book at line-up. Pre-pick different topics and ideas that speak to you in the book and focus on one during each pre-shift. Read it out loud and ask the team what it means to them. Use it as a discussion point to help build the team focus on creating better service. You can also find common threads of feedback you've been receiving from guests and fine tune some action items for your team around similar topics in the book.

- Find one simple phrase, anecdote, or topic in the essays or interviews that makes sense to you and share it with your team. Be specific about how it applies to your specific business or operations and how you would like to apply it to improve service or the work experience.

GLOSSARY OF TERMS

Works Consulted:

Herbst, S.T., Herbst, R. *Food Lover's Companion*. Barron's, 2007.

Colonna-Dashwood, M. *The Coffee Dictionary: An A–Z of Coffee, from Growing & Roasting to Brewing & Tasting*. Chronicle Books, 2017.

Concise Oxford English Dictionary, 11th Edition.

Merriam-Webster's Collegiate Dictionary, 11th Edition.

Organic Certified Coffee in the United States. National Coffee Association, USA.

***

86'd (or 86ed): A phrase used among employees to indicate that the restaurant has run out of a particular item.

2-top: A table set for 2 people

4-top: A table set for 4 people

Acidity: The word *acid* comes from the Latin *acidus*, meaning "sour." All acids are sour to some degree. Sourness (acidity) is found in many natural ingredients such as vinegar (acetic acid), wine (tartaric acid), lemon juice (citric acid), sour-milk products (lactic acid). (*Food Lover's Companion*, 3)

Affogato: A scoop of vanilla gelato or ice cream topped with a shot of hot espresso. Though vanilla is traditional, chocolate gelato is sometimes uses, in which case the dessert becomes affogato mocha. The word *affogato* comes from the Italian *affogare* ("drown"). (*Food Lover's Companion*, 5)

Aerate: To put air into. Usually in reference to steaming milk for foam for coffee drinks. (*Food Lover's Companion*, 8)

Aioli: A strongly flavored garlic mayonnaise from the province region of Southern France.

Allergy: A severe, sometimes life-threatening immune-system reaction. Common sources of food allergies include peanuts, tree nuts, soy, shellfish, fish, sesame, gluten and wheat, eggs, and milk and dairy products.

Appetizer: Usually referred to as the first course of a meal being served.

Arabica: *Coffea Arabica* is the name of the most widely grown coffee species in the world. Arabica itself can be traced back to the Ethiopian highlands. (*The Coffee Dictionary*, 21)

Aroma: A smell or odor that is associated with coffee, food, and other beverages.

Backflushing: Forcing water and a detergent of some sort back up through the espresso machine to clean the passageways of solidified oils and coffee build-up.

Barista: A person who makes espresso and coffee drinks for guests.

Basket: Group handles (the part of the espresso machine that is locked in and released for each shot) can fit a variety of basket sizes, typically ranging from 14g to 22g for couple shots. The individual baskets are designed for a specific dose of coffee to be used. (*The Coffee Dictionary*, 24)

Behind: A phrase commonly used to notify someone that you are walking behind them. Often used in restaurants so people who are multi-tasking can be made aware that you are behind them by saying, "Behind."

Beverage: A liquid that one can drink.

Bland: Not irritating, stimulating, or invigorating. (*Merriam-Webster*, 130)

Blend: A mix of different types of coffee beans that could come from different origins.

BOH: Back of House.

Bun: A sweet or plain small bread. (*Merriam-Webster*, 164)

Biscuit: A small quick bread made from dough that has been rolled out and cut or dropped from a spoon. (*Merriam-Webster*, 126)

Body: Can be described as how big and heavy the coffee feels in your mouth. The body of a coffee will usually be described on a spectrum of light to heavy. (Abbreviated from *The Coffee Dictionary*, 31)

Burning Ice: The process of melting ice so it doesn't sit frozen overnight.

Bussing Tables: Clearing used, dirty, or empty items such as plates, silverware, cups, glasses, and napkins off of a table. Tables should be bussed, cleaned, and reset as soon as a guest has left the table.

Caffeine: A mild stimulant to the nervous system.

Café: A small, unpretentious restaurant.

Call-off: When an employee notifies management that they will not be able to come into work on that specific day.

Campers: Refers to guests who stay at a table long after they are done eating and drinking.

Cappuccino: The cappuccino is possibly the most widely interpreted drink name out there. It is fair to say that a cappuccino is stronger than a latte (there is more coffee than milk) and has a decent amount of foam, though in a lot of commercial shops a cappuccino is just a latte with some chocolate sprinkles added on top. (*The Coffee Dictionary*, 24)

Carry-out: An expression that can be used for picking up food to-go.

Cashier: The position usually responsible for taking the order and payment from the guest.

Chai: Chai is a blend of loose-leaf tea, milk, and ground spices (chai masala), typically cardamon, cinnamon, cloves, ginger, freshly grated nutmeg, and pepper. (*Food Lover's Companion*, 127)

Charcuterie: An assortment of meats; different types of pork, cured meats. Usually presented with cheeses and any other accompaniments such as gherkins, olives, grapes, nuts, etc.

Chemex: A manual pour-over brewing method using a specific one-piece glass vessel.

Chemex papers: Special filter papers used specifically with the Chemex pour-over vessel.

Cherry: The coffee fruit or berry.

Chit: A small piece of paper with writing or typing on it.

Cinnamon: An aromatic spice dried from the inner bark of a cinnamon. (*Merriam-Webster*, 223)

Clopen: A hybrid term of *Close* and *Open*. Usually used when someone works the night before and closes the store and then has to open the store early the next morning, e.g., "I had to Clopen."

Coffee: A beverage made by percolation, infusion, or decoction from the roasted and ground seeds of a coffee plant. (*Merriam-Webster*, 240)

Combo: A term used to refer to an entrée or main dish that comes with a side and/or a drink.

Condiment: Something used to enhance the flavor of food (*Merriam-Webster*, 259), e.g., ketchup, mustard, ranch dressing, sugar, agave.

Corner: Like using the word "Behind" to let someone know you are behind them, many servers use the word "Corner" out loud as they are walking around a corner in the back of the house. This is to let others know you are coming around the corner.

Crema: The darker-colored foam layer on top of a freshly pulled shot of espresso.

Decaffeinated: Having the caffeine removed. (*Merriam-Webster*, 321)

Demitasse: A small cup of black coffee. Can also refer to the cup used to serve it. (*Merriam-Webster*, 331)

Dietary restriction: A non-allergy reason for avoiding certain foods. People might have medical restrictions (e.g., diabetes), religious restrictions (e.g., keeping kosher or halal), or ethical restrictions (e.g., staying vegetarian or vegan).

Doing Inventory: The process of counting all the product in the business at the end of the month.

Doppio: "Double" in Italian.

Dose: Commonly refers to the amount of ground coffee used to prepare a given cup of coffee, though it can also be applied to other aspects such as the amount of water used. (*The Coffee Dictionary*, 72)

Dressing: A sauce—usually cold—used to coat or top salads and some cold vegetable, fish and meat dishes. (*Food Lover's Companion*, 226)

Drip coffee: A common style of coffee brewing, often with an electric appliance, where hot water is slowly drained over coffee grounds through a filter into a carafe below.

Drive-thru: A common way of ordering from a restaurant without leaving your car.

Eat-in: Similar to *Dine-in*. This is when a guest would like to eat their food or drink on the property as opposed to taking it to go.

Entrée: Sometimes referred to as the main course of a meal.

Espresso: It is essentially an intense, highly concentrated coffee beverage of short measure. It is brewed under pressure, which creates a layer of foam on the surface of the drink called the *crema*. (*The Coffee Dictionary*, 79)

Expo: Short for *expeditor*, the person in the kitchen who is in charge of calling out the order tickets, controlling the pace of coursing, and putting the final touches on a plate, ensuring it looks good, before it goes out to the guests.

Extraction: The principles of extraction are really the core concept of any brewing method or coffee-making process. Boil it right down and all cups of coffee are about using some water to take some flavor our of some ground coffee beans. (*The Coffee Dictionary*, 86)

Fair Trade: A movement whose goal is to help producers in developing countries to get a fair price for tier products so as to reduce poverty, provide for the ethical treatment of workers and farmers, and promote environmentally sustainable practices. (Merriam-Webster, 449)

Fast casual: A restaurant where your meal is prepared directly in front of you while you walk down the line or brought to your table after you ordered and paid at the cash register.

Fire: The term "Fire" is used when someone would like a meal to start getting cooked.

First wave: The "first wave" was the commercialization of coffee, mainly defined by mass-market instant coffee.

FOH: Front of House

Food Handler Certification: A certification required in some states for employees who may prepare, store, or serve food.

Fountain drink: Carbonated beverage that comes from a soda fountain.

Franchise: A method of restaurant management, common in fast food and fast-casual dining, in which an operator buys a license to use a larger brand and offer its products.

French press: A classic method of making coffee, usually in a glass vessel. The coffee and water are mixed together and left to steep. A mesh filter is then used to push the coffee grounds to the bottom of the vessel, leaving filtered coffee ready to pour.

Frothing: A process used to create milk foam.

Fryer: A deep utensil used for frying foods. (*Merriam-Webster*, 504)

Full immersion: A brewing method where coffee and water are put together to steep.

Gluten: A substance in wheat flour that produces an allergic reaction in some people.

Green coffee: Unroasted, raw coffee beans.

Grinder: Device operated for grinding coffee beans down into a specific size to be used for an extensive range of brew methods.

Grinding: The process used to grind coffee down to a particular fineness, depending on how easily you would like the water to dissolve the coffee.

Half-and-half: A mixture of whole milk and heavy cream.

Harassment: Unwelcome conduct based on race, color, age, national origin, sexual orientation, gender, religion, ability, or medical/genetic information

Herbal tea: Also known as *tisane*. A tea like drink made by steeping any various herbs, flowers, spices, etc. In boiling water. Such brews have long been used for their calming and rejuvenating qualities. Some of the herbs more commonly used for tisane blends are balm, chamomile, hyssop, mint, and tansy. (Food Lover's Companion, 697)

Hot plate: A simple portable appliance for heating or for cooking in limited spaces. (*Merriam-Webster*, 602)

Hot spot: A place where the customer has the ability to connect wirelessly to the internet.

Inventory: The quantity of goods and materials on hand. (*Merriam-Webster*, 658)

In the weeds: Overwhelmed or too busy to do something else.

Knock box: The container you smash your used espresso grounds into after you are finished pulling a shot of espresso.

The Line: Usually refers to the place in the kitchen where the cooks are lined up preparing food. This would be on the kitchen side of "The Pass."

Low-fat: Referencing a diet or a type of food that contains a low amount of fat.

Maple syrup: A sweet, viscus liquid derived from the sap of maple tree used on breakfast foods such as pancakes, french toast, and waffles.

Menu: A piece of paper with food and drink items for sale listed on it. Also, could be viewed on a board or other surface for customers to see.

Menu count: The amount of items left to sell of a specific item on the menu. This count is usually kept in the Point of Sale system, but can also be found on boards that are visible by employees and updated throughout the shift.

Mocha: A port city in Yemen. This also happens to be a widely varying coffee drink usually made with a combination of espresso, chocolate, and milk.

Michelin star rating: A star rating based on the experience (s) that a Michelin Guide reviewer (s) has had at your restaurant. These ratings are then published in the famous Michelin Guide for selected cities throughout the world. This rating system is different than the reviews/ ratings given by the public on open online platforms.

MOD: Manager on Duty.

Mouth feel: Used by professional tasters as well as foodies, the term mouthfeel describes just that—how a food (such as cheese) or potable (wine or beer) feels in the mouth. Depending on what's being tasted, the descriptors may include everything from "full-bodied" to "light" to "dense." The permutations are endless. (*Food Lover's Companion*, 445)

Muffin: A quick bread made of batter containing egg baked in a pan having cuplike molds. (*Merriam-Webster*, 814)

Mustard: A pungent yellow powder of the seeds of any of several common mustards used as a condiment. (*Merriam-Webster*, 819)

No call/No show: When an employee neither calls off of their work shift or shows up for it.

Nonfat: A product that contains no fat.

No show: A phrase used when a fellow employee, without warning, doesn't show up for their scheduled shift.

On the fly: A term used to mean "right now" or "as soon as possible."

Open faced: Served without a covering layer (as of bread or pastry). (*Merriam-Webster*, 869)

Order-fire: When the kitchen starts cooking an incoming order as soon as it is ordered.

Organic Coffee: A certification under the USDA that provides confirmation that the coffee product has followed a rigorous organic supply chain management process and quality controls from tree to cup, intended to safeguard the organic standards, under the oversight of the USDA Agricultural Marketing Service, which manages the National Organic Program. (NCA, USA)

OSHA: Occupational Safety and Health Administration, which ensures safe and healthful working conditions for workers by setting and enforcing standards and by providing training, outreach education, and assistance. (US Department of Labor)

Panini: Oftentimes refers to a sandwich that is grilled or toasted.

Party: Used to refer the size of a group. A "party" of six.

The Pass: The area in the kitchen that where the cooks pass the recently plated food to the expeditor, runners, or servers.

Pitcher: A vessel from which you pour liquids such as water, juice, or milk.

Policy: Specific guidelines or course of action a company uses to implement rules.

Procedure: The expected standards and processes to accomplish set tasks.

P-Card: A credit card that is used for purchasing goods for the organization or company.

Portafilter: The detachable handle of the espresso machine that holds the basket with coffee grounds and is used for the brewing process.

POS: Point of Sale. Usually refers to the system used in the restaurant to input orders and process payments.

Pour-over: Brewing method where hot water is poured over ground coffee through a filter, extracting flavor through the saturation of grounds, resulting in a cup of coffee.

Pre-Bus: Politely clearing empty items off of a table while the guest is still sitting down. You don't want dirty or empty items such as plates, cups, utensils, and napkins to be lying on the table making it look messy. Pre-Bussing is also considered a part of "Table Maintenance."

QSR: Quick-service restaurant, also known as fast casual.

Quick bread: A sweet or savory bread that is made without yeast.

Ranch dressing: A common salad dressing that is often requested with fries, onion rings, tater tots, other fried foods and sometimes salad.

Roll: A small, usually round, or oblong piece of bread.

Runner: Someone who carries food from the kitchen or pass to the table.

Savory: A term describing food as not sweet but rather piquant and full-flavored. (*Food Lover's Companion*, 606)

Scone: A type of quick bread that can be savory or sweet

Seasonal offerings: Items on a menu that are seasonal based on the time of year, available food products, or holiday promotions.

Second wave: The "second wave" was the emergence of the coffee shops that now dominate the high street, such as Starbucks. This phenomenon occurred in the 1960s in the United States and represented the adoption of the Italian espresso-based drinks culture that drove these businesses. (*The Coffee Dictionary*, 218)

Shake: A beverage resembling a milk shake but made without milk. (*Merriam-Webster*, 1142)

Shelf life: The period of time during which a material may be stored and remain suitable for use. (*Merriam-Webster*, 1147)

Shot: A small amount of espresso that comes from "pulling a shot."

Sides: A small order of prepared food that usually accompanies the main dish.

Side work: Restaurant tasks that you will need to perform to help prepare the restaurant for service. These can be done before, during, or after service. They may include: Filling up condiments, restocking condiment containers, polishing and rolling silver or plastic rolls, restocking items, balancing tables, burning ice and more.

Signature dish: A special dish or dishes that a specific restaurant is known for.

Single origin: A coffee from any single country is technically from a single origin., inasmuch as the coffee is from one country. The coffee, however, could be blend of many diverse coffees from many farms. A number of specialty roasters now have almost exclusively single-origin offerings, and the term in this context is increasingly intended to denote a coffee from a specific variety of coffee plant, from a specific farm. (*The Coffee Dictionary*, 166)

Smoothie: A beverage made by blending fruit with yogurt, milk, or ice cream until it's thick and smooth. (*Food Lover's Companion*, 636)

Specialty coffee: Green coffee (raw and unroasted) that has passed a series of quality high grading evaluations.

Split shift: A shift of working hours divided into two or more working periods (as morning and evening) separated by more than normal periods of time off (as for lunch or rest). (*Merriam-Webster*, 1205)

Steaming: Adding air in the form of steam to milk or other beverages to transform it to foam.

Steam wand: The metal wand hanging off of the expresso machine that is used to steam milk or an alternative beverage.

Standard: An agreed course of action to accomplish a task in a specific way, maintaining a consistent product or service for guests.

Star-rating: Used to grade the product and service of a specific business. These are utilized by many guests as they give reviews or search for reviews on different online platforms. A typical rating would be from 5 stars to 1 star, 5 being the highest for the quality or service grade.

Starter: Another word used for *appetizer* or *first course*.

Steep: To soak tea leaves in hot water. The amount of time a specific tea steeps has an enormous impact on the flavor and tannins extracted from the bag. A longer steep does not necessarily mean more or better flavor.

Sub: Shorthand for substituting an item for another item. Often used if the preparer is out of an item and will substitute something similar. Often used by a customer to ask if a dish can be made with a different ingredient.

Sweet: Having the pleasant taste characteristic of sugar or honey; not salty, sour, or bitter. (*Concise Oxford English Dictionary*, 1455)

Talker: A guest who talks a lot. Who sometimes will keep talking as you are trying to multi-task and do your job. Sometimes this term can be applied to a fellow co-worker.

Tamper: A device, usually round and metal, used to press the coffee grounds down into the basket before loading it into the machine to pull a shot of espresso.

Third-party app: Any app that is used for guests to do business with your restaurant that is not actually owned by the restaurant. Common apps may be used for pickup and delivery.

Third wave: The "third wave" refers to the higher culinary appreciation of coffee and all that this entails: a focus on subtleties of flavor, provenance, and process. (*The Coffee Dictionary*, 218)

Thousand Island: A dressing that can include a mixture of mayonnaise, chili sauce, ketchup, relish, vinegar, and other ingredients.

Tree nuts: Walnuts, pecans, almonds, cashews, macadamia nuts, hazelnuts...any nut that grows on a tree. (Peanuts are not tree nuts—they're legumes that grow in the ground.)

Turning tables: A phrase used in reference to having a group leave a table after a meal and another group sit down at the same table to start their meal.

Variety: Refers to subspecies of the two main coffee species that we grow to make coffee from.

Vegan: A person who does not eat any food made with any animal or dairy products. At times a person may ask, "what vegan options do you have on the menu?" This is one of the reasons it's important to know your menu ingredients very well. (Strict Vegans may avoid products that include honey, eggs, cheese, butter, mayonnaise.)

Vegetarian: A diet avoiding meats and focused on mostly vegetables, fruits, grains, nuts. This diet may include some dairy or egg products as well.

Vendor: A company that offers supplies or products to the restaurant.

Walk-in: A large refrigerator that you can walk into.

Walk-ins: Guests who walk into your restaurant without a reservation.

Yield: We use yield to refer to the resulting cup of coffee. A typical brew recipe will contain two weights: the dose and the yield. The yield refers to the weight of the beverage produced, inclusive of water and dissolved coffee. (*The Coffee Dictionary*, 246)

INDEX

About the Author

Joshua Farrell has worked in the hospitality industry for over 30 years. He started out as a teenager washing dishes in a pizzeria, worked food and beverage counter service jobs, and many years later was a national semi-finalist for a James Beard Award for Outstanding Service with his team in a Michelin-starred restaurant. He has worked as a consultant in leadership, development, and training with a variety of hospitality-focused companies, from small franchises to multimillion dollar corporations. He lives in Los Angeles with his wife, Kirsten, and their two cats, Easy and Mouse.

Acknowledgements

This industry is built on our ability to share our skills, teach each other, and learn from each other. It's one of the aspects of our industry that I'm most proud of. I've worked with some amazing teams behind counters and in restaurants and hotels.

Thank you, Elizabeth Bagby, my editor. You were a delight to work with. Thank you for challenging me to keep at it with fantastic notes and great questions through the edit process.

Thank you, Christo Downs, for your amazing cover design... and stellar music recommendations.

Thank you to the many people who have been incredibly encouraging and helpful in the process of writing this book including Andrew Benator, Hutch Farrell, Marta Lindsey, Davis Campbell, Elizabeth Keliiholokai, Matt Lawler, Robert Hartstein, Jerry Agee, Ken Concepcion, Tim McCracken, Lesley Suter, Ash Roeca, Nick Gallo, and Giovanni Guerrera.

Thank you to the passionate individuals that shared their thoughts with me (and you) in this book. Thank you for taking the time to chop it up with me and share your thoughts on service, life, and the pursuit of excellence. It's these types of discussion that always make me want to do and be better myself.

And most importantly, Kirsten. Thank for all of your support and encouragement through this process and being a great person to ride the river with. I love you.

Printed in the USA
CPSIA information can be obtained
at www.ICGtesting.com
LVHW050823111223
766104LV00002B/103